James Payn

Some Literary Recollections

James Payn

Some Literary Recollections

ISBN/EAN: 9783337217709

Printed in Europe, USA, Canada, Australia, Japan

Cover: Foto ©Thomas Meinert / pixelio.de

More available books at **www.hansebooks.com**

SOME

LITERARY RECOLLECTIONS

BY

JAMES PAYN

AUTHOR OF

'LOST SIR MASSINGBERD' 'BY PROXY' ETC.

A NEW EDITION

LONDON

SMITH, ELDER, & CO., 15 WATERLOO PLACE

1885

TO

LESLIE STEPHEN

A CRITIC BLIND TO NO LITERARY MERIT SAVE HIS OWN

THESE RECOLLECTIONS ARE DEDICATED

BY HIS OLD FRIEND

JAMES PAYN

PREFACE.

THE SUBSTANCE of this book has already appeared under the same title in the 'Cornhill Magazine,' but the work has been recast, and now appears, with additions, in a somewhat different, and, it is hoped, an improved form.

CONTENTS.

SOME LITERARY RECOLLECTIONS.

CHAPTER I.

BOYHOOD—ETON—WOOLWICH ACADEMY—-AT A PRIVATE
TUTOR'S—GETTING INTO PRINT.

ABOVE all writers, I envy and admire autobiographers. Unhappily the feat of narrating one's own life in print can only be performed once. I should like to do it ever so many times, regarding myself in each case from a new standpoint ; but to me it is marvellous how it can be done at all. It doubtless arises from modesty and the total absence of egotism, but for my part I don't remember more than half-a-dozen things that ever happened to me, and still less *when* they happened. There is Scriptural authority for not thinking very highly of the individuals who make a practice of observing ' days and months and times and years,' and

B

so far at least I am a Christian man; but to be able to put every event of one's life into the proper pigeon-hole is nevertheless a gift I envy.

It is necessary, even for the autobiographers, however, to have kept a diary, which unhappily I never did, except for a week or two. I retain a fragment written in boyhood : genuine, but for any benefit I derive from it in the way of assistance to the memory, it might be the Shapira manuscript.

Sunday.—Twice to church. Revs. Jones and Robinson preached. A collection. Sixpence? (I wonder why this note of interrogation.)

Monday.—Wet. Improved my mind. Duck for supper. Tommy. (Who was Tommy? Or was it an ejaculation? The name of a place never mentioned to ears polite is sometimes associated with the word Tommy to express a catastrophe. Perhaps this was an abbreviation.)

Tuesday.—Called on Uncle B.; grumpy and unsociable. Accounts : lucifers and sundries, four pounds.

I suppose I had always a distaste for detail ; at all events I seem to have very soon 'dropped off gorged' from these personal memoranda, the perusal of which makes turbid the stream of life from its very source. I can't even remember who

Uncle B. was ; it was probably a pseudonym for some person in authority of business habits, whose individuality I have forgotten. In the next entry I find a Bishop mentioned.

Wednesday.—(No month, or even year, are ever stated ; the diary seems, like Shakespeare, to have been 'for all time.') The Bishop called.

Did he ? And if so, what did he want ? And who was he ? Our home was not so overrun with Bishops but that I should have remembered him had he been a real one. My conviction is that this also was a pseudonym. Out of such materials as these, though no doubt attractive to the commentator, it is obviously impossible to construct an autobiography. However 'keen to track suggestion to her inmost cell' might be the writer, he could not compress the thing within reasonable limits : if, as usual, there is to be prefixed a narrative of his ancestors during the civil wars (mine were all there) and an ample description of his great-grandmother—from whom he inherited his genius —the work would assume portentous dimensions.

For these reasons, an autobiography (which has been more than once requested from my humble pen) is out of the question. On the other hand, I have certain recollections. My mind,

4 SOME LITERARY RECOLLECTIONS.

though a blank as to dates and even ordinary
details, retains personal impressions vividly enough;
and it is possible in the case of certain noteworthy
persons, with whom during a life of letters I have
come in contact, that my reminiscences of them
may have some interest. They extend, alas! over
many years, but I must premise that I have no
'scandal about Queen Elizabeth,' nor anyone else,
to communicate. This is, I feel, a drawback.
The cry—

> Proclaim the faults they would not show !
> Break lock and seal ; betray the trust ;
> Keep nothing sacred—

goes forth stronger than ever. But unhappily my
memory is so defective that I recollect nothing
against these good folk. There were matters amiss
with them, doubtless, for they were mortal ; but so
far as I was concerned—a very young aspirant to
fame—they gave me of their best. People talk of
the vanity of authors ; of their selfish egotism ;
of their crying out 'Whip behind!' when some
poor fellow would hang on to the footboard of the
chariot in which they themselves ride forth so
triumphantly. But then some people lie. My experience of men and women of letters—which has
been continuous and extends over thirty years— is

that for kindness of heart they have no equals. The profession of healing comprehends, it is true, natures as generous and as gentle, but in that there is (technically speaking) a mixture. I have never known but one absolutely offensive man of letters; and even he was said to be pleasant when sober; though, as I only met him some half-a-dozen times, and his habits were peculiar, I never had a fair chance of finding him in that condition.

As a very young man I remember expressing this rose-coloured view of the calling I had made up my mind to follow to Charles Dickens. He put on that comical look of his—every feature full of humorous significance—and turned to John Forster with 'It is plain our young friend has yet to know ——' And it so happened that I never did know ——, a circumstance which one can hardly regret. 'But,' as the old novelists used to say, 'I am anticipating'—I suppose I must begin at the beginning, and give some account of my early predilection for story-telling and a literary life; though, for my part, I confess that, in perusing the early chapters of similar biographies, I have generally had a tendency to 'skip;' the life of 'literary' boys being very much like that of other boys, with the disadvantage of being generally a miserable

one. Boys with a turn for humour (unless of the
practical joke description) fare worst of all, for
your average boy hates wit even more than other
kinds of intelligence, and licks its possessor with a
wicket, for being ' facetious.'

It was my unhappy lot in youth to have a
lively fancy, and to be much addicted to reading
works of the imagination ; and though I hated
lessons of all kinds as much as any of my contemporaries, they never forgave me this, and it
made me a very unpopular boy. It was hard upon
me, for I suppose in some sort I inherited these
disadvantages. My father was of a genial nature,
very well read, and with a turn for practical matters
also which I never possessed. He had led a life of
leisure for many years, but when it became necessary for him to exert himself for the sake of his
family, he buckled to his work with amazing diligence and success. The necessity I believe arose
from something like disinheritance. In the Town
Hall at Maidenhead there hangs a picture of my
paternal grandfather, in a stiff wig, and with a very
' disinheriting countenance.' He was, at all events,
very rich, and left his only son very far from rich.
At his death my father bestirred himself, and by
help of troops of friends (for he was very popular)

obtained certain appointments; among them the
clerkship to the Thames Commissioners, at that
time an important post with large emoluments
attached to it. He could not, however, have been
entirely absorbed in business, for at the same time
he kept the Berkshire Harriers. I was so young
when I lost him that I have scarcely any remembrance of my father; but he must have been an
attractive man.

Miss Mitford writes to me of him: 'Your father
and I were friends when I was a girl of fifteen, and
he a lad of your own age. I doubt if you know
the manner of man he was, for the cares of the
world had changed him much. In his brilliant
youth he was much like a hero of the fine old
English comedy (which you would do well to
read); the Archers and Mirabels of Farquhar and
Congreve; not a poet, but a true lover of poetry,
with a faculty of reciting verse, which is amongst
the most graceful of all accomplishments.' Almost
my only recollection of my father is our reading
'Macbeth' together; it always fell to my part to
rehearse the dagger scene with a paper-knife. This
I greatly enjoyed, but not so another amusement
which he expected me to appreciate.

Twice a week I had to go hunting; this I

abhorred. I had a nice little bay bony (*Flash of Memory*, 'Lightfoot'), and could ride well enough, but the proceedings were too protracted for my taste, and I wanted to be at home to finish the 'Mysteries of Udolpho' by the fire. There was one thing I disliked even more than hare-hunting. This was fox-hunting. All my family, except myself, had sporting proclivities, and many a time through mistaken friendship have I been given 'a mount' with 'The Craven,' or 'The South Berks,' which I would much rather have declined, had I dared to do so. It was not only my own reputation, however, that was at stake, and I had to go through with it. I remember on one occasion getting some very bad language from a huntsman for feeding some young hounds with cake in a wood. Sometimes the cold, and the waiting about, and the having nothing to read, grew absolutely intolerable ; there was then nothing for it but to dismount, put clover or something in my hair, smear my shoulder with mould, and ride home 'having met with rather a nasty tumble.' Of course it was very wrong ; but why will people compel poor boys to amuse themselves with things that give them no pleasure ? It would have been better (and cheaper) to have let me enjoy 'Peregrine

Pickle,' 'Captain Cook's Voyages,' and the 'Arabian Nights,' all day, without the temptation of practising duplicity. My dearest mother—kindest of women, and at that time one of the most beautiful—was the only human being who understood me. I was a home bird in every feather, and her pet.

Never shall I forget the wretchedness I endured at my first school from home-sickness; fox-hunting was nothing to it. When I used to wake in the mornings, and find myself, after happy dreams, in that land of exile, I thought myself the most miserable of human creatures. I have the keenest recollection of it even now. Nothing that I ever suffered since—and I have suffered like other men, in many ways—has been comparable with the misery of that time. I am well aware, of course, that I was not a fair specimen of the British schoolboy; but when I hear what he calls 'old buffers' talk of the delights of school, and wish themselves back there, I think of the Cretans to whom the Apostle has given the palm for Lying. The author of 'Vice Versâ' has of late, with as much truth as wit, exploded the whole delusion, and I thank him for it. I always learnt my lessons, but without the least interest in them. I pitied and liked the ushers.

The head-master I did not like ; he was a pompous lethargic fellow. I remember on one occasion inquiring of him how Castor and Pollux could have had immortality conferred upon them *alternately*. 'You young fool,' he replied, 'how could they ever have had immortality conferred upon them *at all?*' I was but seven years old, or so, but I perceived from that moment—for how could he otherwise have missed the whole point of my difficulty?—that it was possible for a man to be at once a scholar and an ass. That view has on more than one occasion been since corroborated.

I was only popular at this school for one reason : it was unhappily discovered that I invented stories, and thenceforth—miserable Scheherazadè !—I was compelled to narrate romances out of my own head, at night, till the falling asleep of my last lord and master permitted my weary little body and cudgelled brains to seek the same repose. I remained at this establishment, which was preparatory for ʻEton, for several years. It was so hateful to me (from no fault of its own, I am bound to say ; school was antipathetic to me, that was all), that, when the holidays were over, I used to bury things, which would otherwise have been useful to me, in the garden, so that I might dig them up, when I

returned home, undefiled from any experience of
that classical seminary.

One morning, in the middle of the term, there
was a commotion in the house, to us smaller boys
unintelligible, except that there was no morning
school, which we appreciated as much as the big-
gest. A strange gentleman appeared at midday,
and informed us that the head-master had been
summoned abroad on urgent private affairs, and
that our parents and guardians had been communicated with ; I knew nothing of what it all meant
except that the term had been miraculously and
providentially shortened, and that we were to go
home. Even when I got to learn that the 'urgent
private affairs' meant bankruptcy and flight, I am
afraid I evinced a shocking equanimity, and only
thought of 'Lightfoot' (for it was not the hunting
season) and my mother.

I suppose I was about eleven years old when I
went to Eton. I was at a dame's house, and my
tutor was Cookesley, a very eccentric but capital
fellow. I was probably too young to properly
appreciate even Eton: the fagging, though not
severe, was very offensive to me, and I resented the
ridiculous airs and graces of the upper boys. I
remember a fifth-form young gentleman (looking

in his white tie like a miniature parson) inquiring
of me in a drawling voice, 'Lower Boy, what
might your name be?' Though I never properly
understood the niceties of the Greek aorist, I did
understand the inflections of my native tongue, and
replied, 'Well, it *might* be Beelzebub, but it isn't,'
upon which the duodecimo divine altered his tone
very much, and even proceeded to blows. It was
only the proper punishment for 'cheek,' no doubt,
but I thought it hard that a repartee should be
so ill-received.

The fagging system of which Thackeray has
expressed such bitter scorn was at its height at
that time. Its defenders used to say that it prevented bullying; but, as a matter of fact, where
a fifth-form fellow was a brute, it authorised
it. One B——, a boy at my dame's, was an
especial victim of this tyranny; one of the heads
of the house had taken a particular antipathy to
him, and was always sending him on long errands
for mere cruelty. On one occasion, he sent him to
the end of the Long Walk (four miles away) to
fetch a brick from the statue of George III. A
moralist, or the gentleman in the Society journal
who solves the Hard Questions, may decide what
B—— ought to have done under such circum-

stances. What he did do, was to bring a brick
from a much less distant spot, and take his affidavit
that it came from His Majesty's statue. Whatever
virtues the fagging system may have inculcated, it
certainly taught the Art of Lying. In spite indeed
of the general contempt in which, upon the whole,
I think that vice was held at Eton, there were many
exceptions. Nobody got 'swished,' for example,
if he could evade it by a tarradiddle. Swishing
was, and is, a grossly indecent performance, which
one illustration in the 'London News,' or 'Graphic,'
would assuredly put an end to for ever. Dr. Haw-
trey, who was the head-master in my time, detested
it. I can see him now in his cassock and bands,
holding the birch (as Lamb says of *his* master)
'like a lily,' in his jewelled fingers, while some
young gentleman, in the presence of a troop of
friends, was undoing his braces. 'Please, sir, *first
fault,*' pleads the trembling boy (everybody was let
off the first time, unless for the most heinous
offences). 'I think I remember your name before,'
says the pedagogue in an awful voice.

'My brother, sir,' suggests the culprit. (It was
a happy thing to have had, as I had, a brother
before you—and not too good a boy—at Eton.)

'I'll look at my book,' was the stern rejoinder.

And in the meantime—unless, alas ! he had had no brother before him—the culprit fastened his braces ; he was at least reprieved. A humorous lad I will call Vivian, who had reached the rather unfloggable age of seventeen, and was upon the point of entering the army, was 'swished,' as he thought unjustly, the very week before his departure from the school. In those days a perquisite—and a very large perquisite —of the head-master's was a ten-pound note given to him by every fifth-form boy on leaving. The etiquette was to call at the lodge, and drop the note into a jar, or anything handy, where the doctor could find it, after his dear pupil had gone away. It was something like the visit of a delicate-minded patient to a doctor of medicine. But Vivian only pretended to drop his ten-pound note into the jar, and reserved it for more agreeable purposes. He pictured to himself with great satisfaction the head-master's fruitless hunt after that bit of tissue paper, after he had got over the emotion of wishing him farewell. 'I *can't* flog him for flogging me unjustly,' was his reflection, 'but, dash it, I can fine him !' I have narrated this incident in 'Less Black than We're Painted,' but it is possible that some people (Philistines) may not have read the book.

The cruellest thing that happened to me at

Eton was a vain attempt to contribute to the school magazine, called the 'Eton Bureau;' considering my tender years, however, the disappointment was hardly to be wondered at.

When I had been at Eton a year or so, I received a 'nomination' to the Royal Military Academy and was removed to a preparatory school at Woolwich, where I began my education afresh, and remained many years. In the days when I was young the word 'cramming,' as applied to educational seminaries, was unknown, but the thing itself was in existence, though not on so large a scale as at present. When a boy received a nomination for the Military Academy, though the interval, as in my case, before he could be qualified for admission might be a long one, he was sent at once to one of the many schools at Woolwich, which professed to educate him for that purpose, and for nothing else. Some boys had very little time to spare, and their education (especially if they came from public schools, where little was learnt at that date save Greek and Latin) was necessarily carried on at high pressure. This saved time, and to put the whole establishment on the same footing saved trouble. I had never known what work was till I went to Woolwich, and I had much rather have remained in ignorance. We had

really hardly any playtime, save on Wednesday and
Saturday afternoons, and yet our position was one
of ease and leisure compared with that of boys
at certain rival establishments. At one of them,
where the young gentlemen went especially late—at
fifteen, or fifteen and a half (the age of admission
to the Academy being sixteen)—they took their
lessons with their meals, like dinner pills, and
digested Euclid between the courses. It was taken
for granted (and I am bound to say in most cases
with good reason) that no one who came to Messrs.
Hurry and Crammem's had ever learnt anything
before : yet no explanation of anything was vouchsafed to us. It was understood that we couldn't
swim, yet we were flung out of our depth into the
river of learning. I have tried all systems of education, with the poorest results imaginable, but this one
was certainly the most hateful. For weeks I used
to learn Euclid *by heart*, without a soul to tell me
what was the meaning of it, or why I was punished
for my performances at the board. Languages
have been always as unattainable to me as the
science of music, and for many months I used to
copy my German exercises from a fellow-student,
till a catastrophe happened : I was so ignorant of
the German characters—in which they were written

—that I actually signed his name at the end of one of them, instead of my own. Detection, of course would have taken place much earlier had I been nearer my examination, for the elder boys were looked after sharply enough. Heavens, what a life it was! If a boy had died there, his existence would have ended like that of an ' habitual criminal,' in penal servitude ; and his friends would doubtless have remarked that he had passed away in happy boyhood, before he had known the ills of life. Indeed, I was often told by my elders that I was ' like a young bear, with all my troubles to come.' It is difficult to decide whether your sanctimonious fool, or your philosophic fool, deserves the palm for folly.

What I especially resented at this place was that, in the whirl and hurry of 'cram,' there was no time for reading and writing: for I was in my youth an omnivorous reader, and, in spite of the many mills of education through which (as will be seen) I passed, contrived to learn some things really worth knowing ; it is fair also to say (though I derived little other benefit from these seminaries) that their variety was very use-ful to me, in the line of life I subsequently chose for myself, and offered me a wide study of life

at an unusually early age. As for writing, I was
never tired of setting down 'what I was pleased to
call my thoughts,' on paper, and generally in verse ;
and what is much more strange, I found a channel
(in the eye of the law at least) of ' publication ' for
them. A schoolfellow of mine, Raymond, had a
talent for drawing, and a third scarcely less gifted
genius, Jones, could write like print. These various
talents might have remained comparatively unknown, but for one Barker, who had a genuine
turn for finance, and who hit upon a plan for
combining them. We were like poor and struggling
inventors, who in this young gentleman found their
capitalist, and thanks to him were enabled to
enlighten the world ; and the parallel, as will be
shown, went even further. His idea was that we
should start a weekly paper, full of stories and
poems. I was to compose the contents, Jones was
to write any number of fair copies, and Raymond
was to illustrate them.

' Of course,' said Barker, ' we shall not do it for
nothing,' which I thought (even then) a very just
observation. The price of each copy was accordingly fixed at sixpence. It did not strike me that
anyone would refuse to give so small a sum for such
admirable literature (not to mention the pictures

which indeed I did not think so highly of), but in practice we found there were difficulties. Many boys were of so gross a nature that they preferred to borrow their literature, and spend their sixpences in the tuck shop ; and though the first number (as often happens) was—to Barker—a financial success, the second number fell flat, and there were several surplus copies on our hands. Then came in our proprietor's genius for finance ; he was the treasurer of the school, entrusted with the paying out of a certain weekly pocket-money of two shillings, which, though despised at the beginning of the term when our purses were full, became before the end of it of considerable importance. He resolved on a *coup d'état*, and calmly deducted sixpence from everybody's two shillings, and gave them our paper instead. It was the first instance with which I became acquainted of 'a forced circulation.'

Experiments of a similar kind have been tried by political financiers in many countries, but rarely without great opposition ; ' the masses ' never know what is good for them, and our schoolfellows were no exception to the rule ; they called our proprietor ' a Jew,' and, so to speak, ' murmured against Moses.' He was tall and strong, and fought at least half-a-dozen pitched battles for the maintenance

of his object; I think he persuaded himself, like
Charles I., that he was really in the right, and set
down their opposition to mere 'impatience of
taxation;' but in the end they were 'one too many
for him,' and, indeed, much more than one. He
fell, fighting, no doubt, in the sacred cause of literature, but also for his own sixpences, for we—the
workers—never saw one penny of them.

As I grew older, matters grew better with me
at Messrs. Hurry and Crammem's establishment,
or perhaps the improvement only lay in the fact
that I began to see the humorous side of them. I
learnt to do my work well, though I never liked it,
nor have I ever liked any work except of my own
choosing, though to *that*, Heaven knows, I have
stuck closely enough. The Bohemian side of my
character now began to develop itself, and that so
strongly, that, considering the great respectability of
my family, I am almost inclined to think (like the
Irish hypochondriac) that I must have been changed
at nurse. I used to delight in running up to town on
short leave (from Saturday to Sunday night), and
'in spite of all temptations' of invitations from my
relations, preferred to do so on my own hook. It
was more agreeable to me to be my own master
than to sit in the lap of comfort. At that time 'a

sandwich and a glass of ale '—both, fortunately, of great size—used to be advertised for fourpence, and I have subsisted on that meal, rather than on the stalled ox, and conventionalism therewith. When money has been very 'tight,' I have even slept, I fear, in a day cab, in a mews. At fifteen, in short, I knew more of the queer side of life than many people at fifty, but I became acquainted with it of my own free will, which is a very different thing (and has very different effects) from becoming acquainted with it on compulsion.

I remember going to the Derby, and coming back (from want of funds) a great portion of the journey on an empty hearse, clinging not, indeed, to the plumes, for it had none, but to bare poles. Of course it was all very wrong, but I was never mischievous, nor can I recollect ever having taken the initiative in hurting any living creature. On the other hand, if *I* suffered a gratuitous wrong at the hands of any schoolfellow, and it was not apologised for, I resented it exceedingly: what an innate villain, I reasoned, must he be to attack so harmless an individual ; and I generally contrived not only to be even with the young gentleman in question, but to strike a moderate balance in my own favour.

I have followed this practice throughout life, and, though it is not strictly a Christian virtue, I venture to think it tends to the public advantage. If offensive people could be generally made to understand the theory of the turning of worms, they would be more careful of putting their foot down upon those apparently defenceless creatures. In the matter of reprisals, one is apt, of course, to make mistakes ; but I think, even at that early age, I could recognise the difference between a light-hearted scamp and a cold-blooded scoundrel. That conciliation with the Base, and especially the Cruel, is useless—is a lesson that I learnt as a small boy, and have never forgotten ; I have generally managed—upon principle—to pay them out.

As the time grew near for the entrance examination to Woolwich, Mr. Hurry began, for the first time, to take some interest in me, who had hitherto been left to the ushers. ' Your father ' (he had been deceased for many years) ' has been writing,' he told me, ' very seriously indeed about your Euclid.'

Mr. Hurry knew all the tricks of his trade. He was confident of my passing the ordinary examination, but was very doubtful of my being able to get through the medical branch of it, because I was so very short-sighted. He gave me, however, the best advice. 'They will tell you to look out of the window and describe the colours of the horses on the common. Mind you say "bay," very rapidly, for all horses are either "grey" or "bay."' If not strictly well-principled, Mr. Hurry was very good fun, and I am indebted to him (though I was not aware of it at the time) for much material for my first work, 'The Foster Brothers.'

I thought myself very fortunate (though, as it happened, it eventually came to nothing) when I took the third place at the entrance examination into the Military Academy. The humours of that establishment at that date I shall not attempt to describe ; they were fitted for the pen of a Smollett, but scarcely adapted for a modern audience. I have introduced some of them (after a certain necessary refining process) into 'What He Cost Her,' and the recollection of them has been doubtless of advantage to me, from a literary point of view. *Nihil humanum a me alienum puto* is a motto that belongs to the novelist even more than to the poet ; and, indeed, life at the Military Academy had very little to do with poetry. The government of the place was a despotism, tempered, not by epigrams, but by escapades. Its subjects were

insubordinate, and demanded frequent fusillades—
expulsions. Our age, from fifteen to eighteen, was,
no doubt, a difficult one to legislate for ; we were
neither boys nor men, and though subject to military discipline, like soldiers, we were sometimes
treated quite as small boys. On one occasion, in
order to check extravagance, it was ordained that
we should only have five pounds apiece, of pocket-
money, on rejoining after a vacation ; as one of
us notoriously kept a pack of beagles, this was not
an edict likely to have, at all events, a universal
application.

The authorities feared ridicule quite as much
as the cadets themselves did. I remember the
governor reading prayers to us in the dining-hall,
one wet Sunday. The chapter for the day happened to be the autobiography of St. Paul, in
which the words ' I speak as a fool ' occur more
than once, and those the reader left out, for fear
of exclamations of agreement. It was here that
' Lord Bloomfield ' and ' The Earl of Moira '
(signs of public-houses on Shooter's Hill) were
given by N. as respectable references, and it was
here (or, at least, while he was a cadet) that he
carried out that famous operation in sheep. A
story should never be told twice in print, at all

events by the same man, but, in the interest of those who have not read it, I must be excused for repeating this one.

N. and M., cadets, tall and hairy, and looking much older than they were, found themselves one vacation with only five shillings between them, and in need of capital. They were accustomed to agricultural pursuits, and N. plumed himself on his judgment of sheep. 'Let us go,' he said, ' to the sheep fair at E., and buy a flock and sell them at a profit.' They attired themselves in appropriate raiment and went to the fair ; after a general inspection of the pens, they bought a hundred sheep at 39s. a head—that is to say, they agreed to buy them. M. went with one of the drovers to a public-house, ostensibly to hand him over the money, but really to gain time and to spend his five shillings in treating him, while N. remained with the other to dispose of his bargain at a profit *if he could.* For a whole hour he did no business, but in the end he sold the flock at 40s. a head, realising £5 by the transaction. We talk of a bad quarter of an hour, but here were four of them for poor N. 'Suppose you had *not* sold them,' I said, ' would you not have got into a frightful row ? ' 'Very likely,' he

said. 'All the time I was thinking less of the
buyers than of Botany Bay.' For at that time
we had transportation.

I had some rather amusing experiences of my
own in those Woolwich days, though I am afraid
they did not redound to my credit. There was a
story told (but then people will say anything) of
my preaching on a tub in Hungerford Market, in
order to raise the necessary fund (eightpence) for
the return of self and friend to Woolwich by river
steamer.

I will confess to one adventure, which I suspect
would now-a-days be pronounced of a Bohemian
character. I was returning with a fellow-cadet
one evening in a Hansom cab, when it occurred to
us (for cards we had always with us) to beguile the
journey with a game at cribbage. As it was quite
dusk, we purchased an enormous and highly deco-
rated candle, such as are used for ecclesiastical
celebrations, and stuck it up between us. Having
always a very tender conscience, this gave me an
idea that we were committing a kind of sacrilege,
but there was no help for it. I remember, however, being a good deal startled when an awful
voice, as it seemed from the skies, suddenly thun-
dered down upon us, 'You have forgot his heels.'

It was the cabman, who, interested in the game, which he had been watching through the little door in the roof, thus reminded us of our inadvertence.

My military career, though, as will be admitted, not destitute of incident, was brief; it was cut short, however, not in the usual manner, by expulsion, but by ill health; and at seventeen I was sent to a private tutor's, in preparation for the University.

My school life, as may be gathered, had not been destitute of. fun, but upon the whole I detested it. It was now for the first time that I became acquainted with happiness. To me it is curious that school life should have those attractions, which it certainly possesses for most boys, independent of the imaginary ones with which the glamour of 'the Past' invests it. I suppose the delight they take in sports of all kinds makes up for the discomforts they endure, while, having no particular literary bent, their dry mechanical studies are not more disagreeable to them than any other kind of reading would be. With the exception of what Mrs. Caudle calls 'the fine old athletic game of cribbage,' I, unfortunately, cared nothing for sports; and while I loved poetry and

fiction, the lessons that were imposed upon me
were absolutely hateful. To find myself comparatively my own master, with leisure for my
private pursuits, was, therefore, like escaping from
slavery.

My new tutor was one of the handsomest and
most agreeable men I have ever known, of the
most polished manners and charming social gifts
of all kinds, and his family were as pleasant as
himself. He lived in a large house, once the residence of a great lord, in Devonshire, commanding
the most splendid views. After my previous experience of life, I seemed to myself (not unreason-
ably, I thought, if the theory of compensation was
to be accepted) to have gone to heaven. As a
young man, my new preceptor had been the pet of
the aristocracy ; had been private tutor to more
than one duke, and had educated earls and vis-
counts without number. Many of them had expressed an extravagant regard for him, but their
efforts to benefit him, when he came to need their
assistance, were certainly not extravagant. He was
comparatively a poor man when I first became
acquainted with him, and had the pride which
generally accompanies unaccustomed poverty. He
would have died rather than have asked his noble

friends for anything, and they took great care, as it seemed to me, never to inquire into his circumstances. One of them, a very great magnate indeed, wrote to request his dear old tutor to come up to Scotland and marry him. He did so, and not only received no guerdon from his gushing Grace, but was left to pay his own journey there and back. He never uttered a word of complaint, though I think he felt it ; but it gave me a lesson with regard to the selfish callousness of the rich and powerful (with their motto of *noblesse oblige*, too !), which has never needed—though it has amply received—the corroboration of experience.

The preparation for Cambridge was a mere bagatelle, after what I had been accustomed to in the way of lessons, and though I never cared for University studies, I almost took a pleasure in them for the teacher's sake. I can see myself now doing Euclid with him in his sanctum, without book ; he taught me to carry the figures, even of the sixth book (which are much belettered), in my head, and after a little practice I found no difficulty in it, and even some self-satisfaction.

This, too, was the first and only time in my life that I have derived any pleasure from what seems to please so many people—outdoor exercise.

I had some companions of my own age who taught me the use of the leaping pole, in which I became quite a remarkable proficient. We scoured the country each with a fourteen-foot pole in our hands, and rarely found brook or lane too broad for us. Many a time, like Commodore Trunnion, have I astonished a waggoner by flying from steep bank to bank, over the heads of himself and his horses. I could now, quite as easily, like the cow in the nursery rhyme, fly over the moon.

I have never seen it remarked, with relation to the effect of humour, that, notwithstanding the stupidity of all so-called practical jokes, a material drollery—something incongruous that actually happens—makes a more vivid and lasting impression upon the human mind than anything spoken. It has been my good fortune to have been familiar with more than one great humorist, and to have mixed generally with many utterers of good things. I remember some with great pleasure, but the recollection of them does not tickle me with the same irrepressible mirth as certain humorous *incidents*, which I can never recall, even in the silent watches of the night, without laughter. They owe something of course, to the circumstances under which they took place, and therefore always lose

in the telling ; but to those who have experienced
and can appreciate them they are solid lumps of
delight, which no time can liquefy. One of these
was vouchsafed to me while at my Devonshire
tutor's. I have often told it, but I do not remember
having ever put it into print.

On one occasion we had some private theatricals,
for which a great hall in the centre of the house,
approached by a long passage from the front door,
afforded great facilities. One of the plays was a
dress piece, exhibiting the Court of Queen Elizabeth. It was my frivolous disposition, perhaps,
that caused me to be selected as the Court jester.
A dear friend of mine (since dead, alas! like most
of them) played Sir Walter Raleigh, and I well
remember he took advantage of my being in a
simple network garment to prick my unprotected
limbs with the point of his rapier.

It was a snowy winter's night, and the hall was
crowded with a very large audience, whose servants,
including those of the house, were standing on the
great staircase and in the galleries; and Sir Walter
and I were in the long passage aforesaid waiting to
' come on,' when there came a ring at the front
door. There was no one to answer it, as we knew,
except ourselves. But who, at that time of night,

two hours after the performance had begun, could it possibly be? 'By Jove,' whispered I, already trembling with the sense of the absurdity of what must needs come to pass, 'it's the new pupil!'

My tutor, I knew, was expecting one (from Wales) about that date, but in the hurry and bustle of the theatricals we had clean forgotten all about him. The bell rang again with increased violence. We opened the door, and there stood a little man, with a Bradshaw and a railway rug, just descended from a snow-covered fly. His gaze wandered from the knight in his doublet and hose to the fool in scarlet, and back again, in speechless astonishment. He had evidently a mind to turn and flee, but Sir Walter, with gentle violence, constrained him to enter. We led him along the passage, opened the door of the great hall, and pushed him on to the stage. The applause was deafening. The appearance of a modern railway traveller, with rug and guide among the Court of Elizabeth, was thought to be part of an exquisite burlesque. The Queen wept tears of laughter, the courtiers roared, not from complaisance, but necessity; the whole house 'rose' at the unexpected visitor, who faced it with his mouth open. It was more than a minute before my tutor could understand what had happened.

He came forward full of the politest apologies, marred by fits of uncontrollable mirth.

'My dear Mr. D., I cannot express my sorrow' (which was very true). 'What must you have thought of your reception, and of my house?'

The Welshman was plucky enough, and not unnaturally in a frightful rage. 'I thought it was a lunatic asylum, sir,' he answered bitterly.

Then we gave him three cheers, and one cheer more. The hero of that evening fell at Balaklava a few years afterwards; my tutor and three-fourths of that joyous company have long been dead; but when I think of that inimitable scene, the humour of it sweeps wavelike over all, and for one fleeting minute drowns regret.

The mention of theatricals reminds me that under my tutor's roof I had the pleasure of meeting the once famous Miss O'Neill. She stayed a fortnight in the house with her husband, Sir William Becher. Those, of ripe age, who saw her act used to compare her, and not unfavourably, with Mrs. Siddons. This was the more remarkable since she left the stage on her marriage at a very early age. At the date of which I speak she was between fifty and sixty years of age: a tall, commanding-looking woman, with a certain majesty in her mien and movements. She talked of 'the Garden' and 'the Lane,' and was very fond of recitation. I remember her giving us 'Hohenlinden,' one afternoon in the hall, in very fine style.

It was when I was a pupil in Devonshire that the meadows of manuscript which I had written began to produce their first scanty crop of print.

A curious chapter might be written concerning the channels through which authors have first addressed the public. From the nature of the case, they have been mostly of a humble kind. One rarely writes for the 'Times' or the 'Edinburgh' at seventeen, or rather, though we may write *for* them (for young gentlemen of the pen are audacious enough), one's lucubrations are first 'accepted' in much more modest regions. Thackeray told me that the first money he had ever received in literature (under what circumstances he did not say, but they must have been droll ones) was from Mr. G. W. M. Reynolds. For my own part, I may, so far, have been said to have been born with a silver spoon in my mouth, for my literary godfather was no less a person than Leigh Hunt. In the flesh, I regret to say, I never knew him ; but as a boy I had an admiration for him that was akin to love. I suppose no writer has ever preached the love of books so eloquently as he has done, or gained more disciples. He had a most kind and gracious nature, which was cultivated to extremity ; culture is much more common nowadays than it was in his time, but unless the nature of the soil is gracious, very little comes of such 'top dressing.' Leigh Hunt combined with the 'fine brain' the tenderest of human hearts. His ignorance of business matters and his poverty made him to natures of the baser sort an object of ridicule. Carlyle used to keep three sovereigns in a little packet on his mantelpiece, which he called ' Leigh Hunt's sovereigns,' because he occasionally lent them to him, and was wont to narrate the circumstance to all whom it did *not* concern. Hunt would have lent *him* three thousand sovereigns, had he possessed them, and never disclosed the circumstance.

There was nothing in his literary life which Dickens regretted so much as the unintentional wrong he did Leigh Hunt in his portrait of Harold Skimpole. It was true that he drew one side of it from his friend, but the other side—the selfishness and the baseness—had nought to do with him. They were indeed so utterly opposed to his character, that it perhaps seemed to Dickens that no one could associate them with the original of the picture.

Nothing is more common than for a novelist to paint in this way, and for the very purpose of the concealment of identity ; but in this case the likeness was, in some points, too striking to escape recognition, and the others were taken for granted, whereat both painter and sitter were cruelly pained.

, The first composition of my own which I had the bliss to see in print was a little poem called 'The Poet's Death '—a queer subject enough to *begin* a poetical career with—published in ' Leigh Hunt's Journal,' one of the many periodicals which owed their being to his sanguine temperament and the optimism of a publisher. It had a short life, and I am afraid not a merry one. Soon after, I wrote a series of ' Ballads from English History,' in ' Bentley's Miscellany,' of which I think, at that time, Harrison Ainsworth was the proprietor and editor. When I ventured, after half a dozen of them, or so, had made their appearance, to hint at payment, I received a note from Mr. Ainsworth explaining that 'the circumstances of the magazine were such that it could afford no *pecuniary* remuneration to its contributors.' The word ' pecuniary ' was italicised, as though I had received some remuneration of another kind. If I had had to trust to my muse for subsistence (though upon

my word I still think I wrote very pretty poems),
I should have died early unless some Dr. Tanner
had communicated to me his secret of living without food.   One of the few poems I ever got paid
for was a humorous one which I had the pleasure
to see the other day quoted in an American collection of 'anonymous and dead authors.'   It was
written upon a great friend of my boyhood, a
pointer called 'Jock.'

> A rollicksome, frolicsome rare old cock
> As ever did nothing was our dog Jock ;
> A gleesome, fleasome, affectionate beast,
> As slow at a fight, as swift at a feast ;
> A wit among dogs, when his life 'gan fail,
> One couldn't but see the old wag in his tale,
> When his years grew long and his eyes grew dim,
> And his course of bark could not strengthen him.
> Never more now shall our knees be press'd
> By his dear old chops in their slobbery rest,
> Nor our mirth be stirr'd at his solemn looks
> As wise, and as dull, as divinity books.
> Our old friend's dead, but we all well know
> He's gone to the kennels where the good dogs go,
> Where the cooks be not, but the beef-bones be,
> And his old head never need turn for a flea.

The proprietor of the object of this eulogy was
so pleased with it that he placed it over the dog's

tombstone, and much to his annoyance found he
had a great deal more to pay the stonecutter than
I had received for the original manuscript. In
short, though at that time of my life, and long
afterwards, I much preferred verse to prose, it soon
became manifest to me that poetry would, in my
case, be its own reward.

My first prose article found acceptance in
' Household Words.' It was the forerunner of
scores and scores contributed to the same periodical, but no other gave me a tithe of the pleasure
this one did. A mother's pride in seeing her first-
born in long clothes is no doubt considerable, but
it is nothing to an author's delight upon the appearance of his first article in print. In this case,
the well-known line, ' Half is his, and half is thine,'
does not apply : the little creature is his very own,
and, small as it is, plays the part of master of the
ceremonies in introducing him to the world at
large. From that moment he is no longer a
private person, but an author. I don't know how
many attempts I had made to obtain that *status*
before I succeeded ; the perseverance of Bruce's
spider as compared with mine was mere impatience. If I could have foreseen how long it would
be before I was fated to be successful again my

happiness would have been not a little dashed ; but as it was I was in the seventh heaven. Up to this day, when I look back upon the letter I received, announcing the acceptance of 'Gentleman Cadet' (a short sketch of life at the Academy), it awakens emotions. The writer was W. H. Wills, who assisted Dickens in his editorship, a man of kindly nature and (of this I was especially convinced just then) of excellent judgment. He was devoted to his chief, conscientious to his contributors, and an excellent fellow, as I had afterwards good reason to know ; but it was a disappointment to me that I had not heard from 'the Master' himself. Even that, however, I almost forgot when I received the *honorarium* (three guineas) for my little paper. It seemed to me that fame and fortune had both opened wide their gates to me at once. A lady novelist has written rapturously of the feelings that were aroused within her by the first kiss from her beloved object, though he was but a Detrimental ; I felt like her, with the additional satisfaction of believing myself to have made an excellent match.

The first question that occurred to me was, What should I do with the money ? It was a sum too small to invest, and too sacred to be frittered away : in the end I bought a pig with it. This requires a note of explanation. In Devonshire there are no pigs worthy of the name, only a kind of dog with a pigskin on it—a circumstance which much distressed my tutor, who was a judge of pigs, and admired them exceedingly. Accordingly, when I returned after my next vacation, I bought him a genuine specimen of the animal from Berkshire. Though country born and country bred, I was always extremely ignorant of country matters ; a fine landscape delighted me, yet I scarcely knew an ash from an elm ; and though I liked animals, I did so as a child likes them, without knowledge of their habits. To this day one of my objections to visiting at country houses is that so many of their owners compel one to feel an interest in their horses and cattle. 'Perhaps you would like to see the stables,' &c. All that I have always hated, and of course I knew nothing about pigs.

The animal in question was chosen for me by an expert, and he (the animal) accompanied me, in a large hamper, by train to Devonshire. It was a very hot day in August, and it struck me, as I got out at Bristol for some liquid refreshment, that the poor pig must be thirsty too. I am now aware that it was an error in judgment, but it arose from

a natural tenderness of heart. We had ten minutes
to wait, but it was with some difficulty that I obtained the services of a porter for this (probably
unique) performance. The station was in a state
of great confusion ; two excursion trains had come
in, and there was a cattle market below stairs, he
told me. However, we got my hamper and took
it down in the lift to an unoccupied apartment ;
my four-footed friend never uttered a sound during
this process—he was either dazed with unwonted
travel, or preparing himself for some coming
struggle ; but I regarded him with the tenderest
sympathy, believing him to be half dead with heat
and drought. The porter procured a pan of water,
and then proceeded to open the hamper. What
took place next I cannot describe, for it happened
in a mere flash of time : there was a cry of panic,
rage, and fear—a squeal is no word for it—a
broken pan, a prostrate porter, and a mad pig
gone ! If the door had been closed, he would
without doubt have bitten us both, but fortunately
the man had left it open. The next moment the
creature was in the market—the 'open market,' as
it is called, but altogether out of *my* reach. He
had joined a great band of pigs (though the owner
denied it), and identification was out of the question.

Such was the fate of the pecuniary proceeds of my first article.

In other respects, however, it was more fortunate ; it made some little stir in the periodical world, and even in one region which may be fairly said to be remote from it. It came under the notice of the Governor of the Woolwich Academy, who wrote to Dickens upon the subject, with some acerbity. When the faults of any educational establishment are indicated, I have always noticed that he who points them out is the subject of one of two kinds of attack. 1. If he has been there in person he ought to be ashamed of himself for suggesting that it falls short of perfection ; he is a bird that fouls its own nest. 2. If by some slight inaccuracy of detail he betrays that he has received his information at second hand, then he knows nothing about it.

'If your correspondent had been a cadet himself,' wrote the general, 'I should net have addressed you, but it is clear to me that he is an outsider.' A courteous reply informed him that the writer of the article *had* been a cadet, on which the governor— evidently still in doubt—demanded his name. This was a course which, unless he had reason to believe he had been wilfully deceived, Charles Dickens was the last man to adopt, with respect to any con-

tributor, without permission, and he wrote to me
to ask it. It was the first of many letters that I
have received from that kind and gracious hand,
but none have given me so exquisite a pleasure. I
was fortunately able to reply to his communication
in a manner that not only satisfied himself, but the
irascible general ; and thus began an acquaintance
which presently ripened into friendship, none the
less sincere though the obligations in connection
with it were, from first to last, all on one side.

CHAPTER II.

COLLEGE LIFE—W. G. CLARK—DR. WHEWELL.—
DE QUINCEY—GEORGE BRIMLEY.

IT is generally understood—I suppose from their
each forming a part of our educational career—
that the difference between school life and college
life is (literally) one only of degree. This is by no
means the case ; it is greater even than the dis-
similarity so much insisted upon between life at
college and that in the world beyond it. The
undergraduate, though he may be far indeed from
having reached years of discretion, is his own
master, and has his time almost wholly—save the
necessity of keeping certain lectures and chapels—
at his own disposal. Even the chapels, I believe,
may now be omitted if the young gentleman is
'advanced' enough in his ideas to entertain a conscientious scepticism ; but even in my time we were
free enough, and the relief from the discipline and
the restraints of school was to me like a manu-
mission from slavery. One's whole surroundings

wear quite another aspect, and even the same
young men whom one has known as boys often
present quite a different nature, which is, in fact,
their true one. This is not so much the case, indeed, with 'reading men,' who, keeping the same
end in view which they had at first, preserve to a
great extent the same characteristics ; but for the
rest of us, though for the first term the old associations may linger and exercise some influence, we
soon drift away from the loose bond which bound
us to our school companions, and, keeping a few of
them for future intimacy, choose our friends from
the university world for ourselves by a natural
selection derived from common pursuits and pleasures. I am afraid that pleasure had a good deal
to do with my selection, and I don't regret it, for
some of those friends are as dear to me as ever.
It is a mistake to suppose that all pleasure is
necessarily selfish, or that the intimacies arising
from it vanish like ' friendships made in wine.'

At this time also, thanks to my literary proclivities, I made acquaintance with persons of high
university standing in my college (Trinity) who
would otherwise have been out of the reach of an
undergraduate who cultivated neither the classics
nor the mathematics. My performances in the

lecture-room or in the examinations would certainly not have recommended me to their notice—
the road of academical distinction which usually
leads to the favour of the dons was closed against
me—but the publication of a little volume of
poems ('Stories from Boccaccio') introduced me
to such of them as in my eyes were most worth
knowing, as it were, by a short cut.

These gentlemen, of course, were not merely
scholars, but men of wide human sympathies, to
whom (to put an old joke into a new bottle) the
particle *de* was not so absorbing as to shut out all
interest in the particle *men*. Among them I especially mention W. G. Clark, one of the most
accomplished and deservedly popular of men. As
Tutor of Trinity, and afterwards as Public Orator,
he had a wide university reputation; as the author of 'Gazpacho' and editor of the Cambridge
Shakespeare, he was known to the world without;
but only those who had the privilege of his friendship could understand that magic of manner and
charm of conversation which caused the late Lord
Clarendon to waive his own acknowledged claim
to be 'the best of all good company' in his favour.
'I think W. G. Clark,' he said, 'the most agreeable
fellow—and he did not mean fellow of a college

only—I have ever met.' **Clark** was a conversationalist of the highest order, and the rarest. Wits are still to be met with now and then ; good *raconteurs* are not uncommon—some of whom even bring in their anecdotes in a natural manner, and not by the head and shoulders—but as a rule they are too much given to monologue.

Lever was a man of this kind—bright, genial, cheery, and full of good stories ; he pleased one like an embodiment of his own creations, but he did not —in my judgment at least—understand conversation. I know men, also, who may be said to be too good talkers. Their words are so well chosen, and their periods so rounded, that to listen to them is like listening to somebody reading aloud ; they hold you with their mellifluous utterances so long that before they reach the end of their league-long sentence (the finale of which one can nevertheless clearly foresee) you have forgotten what you wished to reply to it. Clark had none of these faults ; he had not only the means of pleasing, far beyond what are possessed by most good talkers, but what is often wanting in them, the desire to please. Nor do I remember, among the many bright and pungent sayings that fell from his lips, a single one that had a sting in its tail.

A characteristic retort of his just occurs to me, which, though of a personal nature, can assuredly wound nobody by repetition. One of the Trinity dons, though known to the world of learning as the greatest of living Latin scholars, was, from his gentleness and good nature, disrespectfully dubbed by his intimates and associates 'the Ox.' One night, after dining at the Master's 'Lodge,' he happened to drop into Clark's room, and began to speak of the occurrences of the evening. There had been some discussion, he said, about Plato, and it was clear to him, from the Master's observations, that he had been indebted to certain ideas upon the subject to Mr. Llewellyn Davies' recent translation of that author. 'Ah,' said Clark, with that quiet smile which always fell short of the merits of the sally it heralded, 'the Ox knoweth his Master's Crib.'

Fortune has thrown me among a good many bright talkers during my life, but I don't think I ever heard a wittier thing, even from W. G. Clark himself. He was the Amphitryon of Trinity, and at his table I first learnt what that which Dr. Johnson used to call 'good talk' was like.

To the Master (Whewell) I was also personally introduced through the medium of my turn for

verse-making; the incident, however, was not altogether to my credit, and reminds one of the ill-
considered boast of the gentleman to whom the
king had spoken, but, as it turned out, in no very
complimentary way. At college, of course, are
retained

> All usages thoroughly worn out,
> The souls of them fumed forth, the heart of them torn
> out,

and, among others, that of commemorating the Re-
storation of his Most Christian Majesty Charles II.
Finding on the hall 'screens' one 29th of May an
account of the celebration for the day in Latin, I
ventured to write with my pencil some extempora-
neous lines on the subject immediately after the
word *gratiâ* :

> For the sake of him who sold
> Dunkirk to the French,
> And gave away the gold
> To a naughty little wench.

While I was still contemplating (and doubtless
with some youthful vanity) this inspiration of my
muse, the screen became darkened by an enormous
shadow, and to my extreme horror I perceived the
Master reading over my shoulder this revolutionary

E

effusion. His grim face never relaxed, though I
had afterwards reason to believe he was tickled.
'That screen, young gentleman,' he observed in
awful tones, 'is not intended for the publication of
your political sentiments.' He at once gave orders
for the obnoxious epigram to be removed, and for
my part I was thankful that they were not for my
immediate execution.

The great Doctor was not, in undergraduate
eyes—or, at all events, in the eyes of those like
myself who were about 'only not to disgrace themselves by taking an ordinary degree'—an agreeable person. His manners were rough, and his
temper, when he troubled himself to keep it at all,
of the shortest.[1]   I remember his looking out of a
window of 'the Lodge' to address the head of the
police on some occasion when the great square
was *en fête* for some Royal visit, and noting how
very short it was. The inspector was at some
distance off, and the fall of the fountain drowned
the Master's voice, so that he did not hear it.

'Mr. Inspector Tanner!' This was delivered

[1] It is fair to state that my view of Dr. Whewell's character
was merely an undergraduate one. Friends of my own time, who
had entertained the same view, took a very different and much
more favourable one of him on later acquaintance. I am assured
by them that he had a large and generous disposition, and that the
rough husk contained a tender kernel.

very courteously, just as Mr. Chucks the Boatswain used to begin all *his* allocutions.

'Inspector Tanner!' Here the prefix was significantly omitted, and the voice grew perceptibly harsher; still no answer.

'Tanner!' The faintest trace of civility was now dropped; Tanner might have been the name of a bull pup who would not come to heel.

' *You there !* ' was the final appeal delivered in the tone of a screech-owl. Every note of the brief gamut had been run through in about ten seconds.

Whewell had quite a sublime manner, supplemented by a Northern burr of expressing contempt, but it was often misapplied. His criticism upon Tennyson's 'Northern Farmer' was an example of it.

'It seems to me that the poet has wasted a great deal of dialectic ingenuity in describing a very *wuthless pussonage.*'

Most people in his eyes were *wuthless* who were not acquainted with the Inductive Sciences. His presence was majestic, he made an admirable figure-head for the collegiate ship; but, though I speak of course as a cabin boy, I never heard of his troubling himself about the crew.

His sayings, however, were 'extremely quoted.' I remember one (it was, at least, always attributed to him) which struck me as admirable; I have never heard it since, and it may be forgotten, which it does not deserve to be. He was at that time in controversy with Sir David Brewster about the plurality of worlds, and took, as is well known, the view that there was but one world, as was very natural, considering the prominent place he occupied in it.

Some one slyly pointed out to him the passage in the Vulgate, *Nonne erant decem mundi?* To which he instantly replied, 'Very true, but look at the next question, *Ubi sunt novem?*'[1]

My acquaintance with Thomas Chenery, the late editor of the 'Times,' with whom I became afterwards long and intimately connected, began at Cambridge. We belonged to the same Shakespeare club and many times heard the chimes at midnight (from a good many churches) together. The same tenderness and consideration for others distinguished him then which were his attributes in later life, and endeared him to all with whom he was

---

[1] For the benefit of the 'country gentleman' and the ladies whose shortcomings upon such matters I sympathise with and share, it may be well to state that the word 'mundus' stands for both 'the world' and 'cleansed.'

brought into contact. A man even then of some reticence and reserve of manner, unusual in youth, but which once broken through revealed one of the kindest of human hearts. I am glad here to acknowledge, what he himself would have been slow to admit (for he never remembered his own kindnesses), that I am under great and lasting obligations to him.

Life at Cambridge in my time was admirably described both by pen and pencil; author and artist were, however, rather my seniors, and to my own loss I did not become acquainted with them till after I left college. The author was J. Delaware Lewis, whose 'Sketches of Cantabs' is to my mind the liveliest little book ever written by an undergraduate; its keenness of observation greatly impressed Dickens, who told me that he had applied to him in consequence to write for 'Household Words,' and added that it was the only case in which he had ever done so. The artist was John Roget, whose 'Language of Mathematics' and 'Cambridge Sketch-book' were the delight of my Cambridge contemporaries.

Undergraduates who feel some wish to distinguish themselves, but to whom the studies of the University are not attractive, generally turn

their attention to oratory, for the exhibition of
which the debates at the ' Union ' give great opportunity, and if I came under any particular heading
in Mr. Lewis's classification of his fellow-students,
it was that of ' the Unionic Cantab.'

The debates were almost always upon political
subjects, and I remember having had the hardihood
on one occasion to place upon the notice board a
proposition for the sweeping away of the hereditary aristocracy of our native land, which created
no little sensation ; there was an immense audience,
but those who came to laugh remained, I fear, to
carry out their intention, since the motion had but
eight supporters. Last year, I note that the same
proposition gained one hundred votes, which shows
that, though opinion at college moves like the
tortoise, it does move ; at school, its motion, if it
moves at all, is that of a glacier—imperceptible.

Charming as is undergraduate life at college,
with its youth, and health, and freedom from cark-
ing cares, it is outdone by the joys of a reading
party in the long vacation—especially when you
yourself have no intention of reading. I joined
such a party in my second year, at Inverary, not
without invitation from the authorities (its two
' coaches ') of course, but very little I fear to its

advantage. When I had done with my own light[1] studies, which was comparatively early in the day, I became what the mathematical coach termed 'a disturbing element.' I was like the boy in the fable who, having a holiday on his hands, requested the diligent animals to play with him ; but we differed in this respect—in my case they consented. ' I lost eight places in the tripos through that fellow,' one of them was once heard to murmur, in subsequent deprecation of poor me. The idea of the tripos at Inverary indeed seemed preposterous ; it was such 'a far cry' from Loch Awe. It should now be a comfort to him to reflect that his friendship doubled for me the charms of that delightful spot, and assisted the growth of my ideas.

For twenty years to come it was my custom to visit, every summer, some picturesque locality, which I have always found to give freshness to my pen, but nothing ever surpassed that time at Inverary.

> Dhuloch, Queen of inland waters,
>   Virgin yet so near allied ;
> Morn and eve with plaint and tremor
>   Sought for Ocean's bride ;

---

[1] With Englishmen all literature in their own language is called 'light.' Shakespeare is light ; Æschylus, Euripides, and even Aristophanes, are deemed not heavy of course (Heavens !), but serious.

> Never more I woo thine echoes,
> .Never let the oar blades glance,
> Lightly as the wings of heron,
> Not to break thy trance.

Those days are gone, those places I shall never revisit, but they still abide with me.

> My heart leaps back to rock and fell,
> The bridge, the quai, the streets uprise
> To glass themselves in tearful eyes,
> And all the haunts we loved so well.

In the ensuing summer, after the publication of another volume of poems, I visited Edinburgh and called upon De Quincey, to whom I had a letter of introduction from Miss Mitford. He was at that time residing at Lasswade, a few miles from the town, and I went thither by coach. He lived a secluded life, and even at that date had become to the world a name, rather than a real personage ; but it was a great name. Considerable alarm agitated my youthful heart as I drew near the house : I felt like Burns on the occasion when he was first about ' to dinner wi' a Lord ;' it was a great honour, but something rather to be talked about afterwards than to be enjoyed in itself. There were passages in De Quincey's writings which

showed that the English opium-eater was not
always in a dreamy state, but could be severe and
satirical. My apprehensions, however, proved to
be utterly groundless, for a more gracious and
genial personage I never met. Picture to yourself
a very diminutive man, carelessly—very carelessly
—dressed ; a face lined, careworn, and so expres-
sionless that it reminded one of 'that chill change-
less brow, where cold Obstruction's apathy appals
the gazing mourner's heart'—a face like death in
life. The instant he began to speak, however, it
lit up as though by electric light ; this came from
his marvellous eyes, brighter and more intelligent
(though by fits) than I have ever seen in any other
mortal. They seemed to me to glow with eloquence.
He spoke of my introducer, of Cambridge, of the
Lake Country, and of English poets. Each theme
was interesting to me, but made infinitely more so
by some apt personal reminiscence. As for the
last-named subject, it was like talking of the
Olympian gods to one not only cradled in their
creed, but who had mingled with them, himself
half an immortal.

The announcement of luncheon was perhaps
for the first time in my young life unwelcome to me.
Miss De Quincey did the honours with gracious

hospitality, pleased, I think, to find that her father had so rapt a listener. I was asked what wine I would take, and not caring which it was, I was about to pour myself out a glass from the decanter that stood next to me. 'You must not take that,' whispered my hostess, 'it is not port wine, as you think.' It was in fact laudanum, to which De Quincey presently helped himself with the greatest *sang froid.* I regarded him aghast, with much the same feelings as those with which he himself had watched the Malay at Grasmere eat the cake of opium, and with the same harmless result. The liquor seemed to stimulate rather than dull his eloquence. As I took my leave, after a most enjoyable interview, to meet the coach, I asked him whether he ever came by it into Edinburgh.

'What !' he answered, in a tone of extreme surprise ; 'by coach ? Certainly not.'

I was not aware of his peculiarities : but the association of commonplace people and their pointless observations were in fact intolerable to him. They did not bore him in the ordinary sense, but seemed, as it were, to outrage his mind. To me, to whom the study of human nature in any form had become even then attractive, this was unintelligible, and I suppose I showed it in my face, for he proceeded to explain matters. 'Some years ago,' he said, 'I was standing on the pier at Tarbet, on Loch Lomond, waiting for the steamer. A stout old lady joined me ; I felt that she would presently address me ; and she did. Pointing to the smoke of the steamer which was making itself seen above the next headland, "There she comes," she said. "La, sir ! if you and I had seen that fifty years ago, how wonderful we should have thought it!" Now the same sort of thing,' added my host with a shiver, 'might happen to me any day, and that is why I always avoid a public conveyance.'

My interview with De Quincey I was not likely to forget, but I never flattered myself that he would have any remembrance of his youthful visitor. A few years afterwards, however, I received from him an entire edition of his works, with a most gracious allusion (in the 'Autobiographical Sketches') to my poems. 'The Story of the Student of St. Bees,' he says, 'has been made the subject of a separate poem by my friend Mr. James Payn of Trinity College. The volume contains thoughts of great beauty, too likely to escape the vapid and irreflective reader.' This good-natured eulogy rang in my ears for many a day, nor did my college friends forget, at all events, one portion of it : with a

monstrous misapplication of terms, they hencefor-
ward dubbed me 'the vapid and irreflective reader.'
I remember my mother showing, with pardonable
pride, this criticism of De Quincey to a Dean of the
English Church, who was then at the head of the
High Church party at Oxford. 'Very flattering to
your son, madam, no doubt,' he said ; 'but who *is*
this Mr. De Quincey ? '

Such ignorance was of course unpardonable in
my eyes, but it is quite amazing how ignorant so-
called scholars often are of matters connected with
the literature of their own country ; in many cases
they even fail to understand its beauties when they
are pointed out to them, while, on the other hand,
anything written in a dead language, however dull
and poor, they value at a fancy price. I was at
that time undergoing the infliction of 'The Seven
Against Thebes' in the Trinity lecture-room ; the
play was introduced to us under the most favourable
circumstances, for W. G. Clark was our lecturer,
who had the art of illustrating everything he had
to discourse upon in the happiest manner ; but
nothing could conceal its dulness. I questioned
him in private as to what he really thought of it.
' Do, pray, be honest with me,' I said ; 'the play is
by Æschylus, I know, but is it not rubbish ? '

'It is certainly not his masterpiece,' was all I could get out of him, accompanied, however, with a droop of the eye that spoke volumes. It was hardly to be expected that an augur should have been more frank save to another augur.

In addition to my two volumes of poems, I wrote while at Cambridge for various periodicals ; more often *for* them than *in* them. The article I had written in 'Household Words' no doubt owed its acceptance to the peculiar information it afforded rather than to its literary merits, and for a long time I endured continuous rejection from that quarter. It may be of some comfort to youthful aspirants to hear that in one year I had six-and-twenty articles rejected by various 'organs.' Improved and enlarged, they have all since seen the light, but in those early years disappointment was my constant mate ; it was never, however, checkmate. I always felt that I had something to tell worth hearing, if I only knew how to tell it, and could get anybody (an editor) to listen to me. I wrote in all sorts of ephemeral magazines ; one of them, the 'Welcome Guest,' published a paper of mine on college life, called 'My Degree,' which was placarded on all the walls of Cambridge. That I thought was fame indeed, and I was probably neither the first nor the last who has confused reputation with advertisement.

The first notice I ever had in a newspaper was a review of my 'Stories from Boccaccio,' by George Brimley (at that time the Librarian of Trinity), which appeared in the 'Spectator;' it was thirty years ago, but I have not forgotten it, nor the writer.   It was like ten thousand tonics, in a single dose ; when I became a reviewer myself, and had to deal with a young author who had genuine merit in him, I never failed to recall the encouragement I had myself received when I most needed it.   It is very easy to be scathing ; but if even a morose-natured man could be aware of the torture he inflicts—how with that easy wheel of his 'he sets sharp racks at work to pinch and peel'—he would mingle a little of the milk of human kindness with his gall : even if he be not conscious of having ever possessed literary merit himself, he has at least been young and can remember the sensitiveness of youth.   Let him spoil the rod on the author of well-seasoned skin (on *me*, if he likes, and welcome), but spare the child.

Reviewers, who are popularly supposed to be the young author's enemies, are generally quite the reverse.   Their power to injure merit, where it

really exists, has been absurdly exaggerated, but
not more than their will. The best of them are
often authors themselves, who (notwithstanding
the popular sneer) have *not* failed in authorship ;
and the same circumstances—the love of books
and the society of genial and cultured folk—which
mollify the mind of authors and prevent them
from becoming ferocious, have the same effect
upon themselves. For my part, with here and
there the exception of some young gentleman
trying his prentice hand in not very high-class
literary organs, I have always found reviewers at
least as quick to appreciate as to condemn.

There was a Mormon community in my time
at Cambridge which interested me. I sometimes
attended their chapel, and became acquainted with
one of their elders, whom I do not think was a
rogue. At all events, he did not take advantage
of his creed, for so far from having a plurality of
wives, he had not even one. He had not the
faintest spark of humour in his composition, but
one of his statements greatly tickled me. He
professed to have a great reverence for the Holy
Scriptures, to which Mr. Joe Smith's book was, in
his view, the supplement. I asked him how he
got over the text, ' If any man shall add unto

these things,' &c.   He reflected for a moment, and then replied, ' That refers to the Commentators.'

I have forgotten to say that after leaving Woolwich I was intended for the Church, so that my attendance at the Mormon Chapel arose from no lapse from orthodoxy.   It was only that I was desirous of becoming acquainted with every phase of human nature. ' I attended in due course the theological lectures, but the recollection of them has vanished ; the ' dust of creeds ' seems to have confused me, to judge by an old examination paper which I came across the other day, on the back of which a few crude elements of faith are written in verse.   One of them runs :—

I believe in the fat Johnian whose face in the sun doth shine,
And who, not looking in the least like a human being, I conclude to be divine.

This could hardly have been a serious confession of faith.

I took my degree, however—a first-class ' Poll,' which my good folks at home believed to be an honourable distinction.   I learnt very quickly what little was required for this purpose, but it all passed away like water from a duck's back.   Greek was always 'Greek' to me, and its grammar I detested with a hatred that I find it difficult to feel even for my personal enemies; there was the less excuse for me, as I certainly knew little about it.

I remember dining with one of the examiners after my work in the Senate House was over, who was telling stories about the examinations of the previous day. 'There is one young gentleman,' he said, 'who, if he does not know more about mathematics than classics, will most assuredly be plucked. He has declined μέγας as if it were a participle, μέγας, μέγασα, μέγαν.' The table was in a roar, and it was agreed on all hands that, however he did the other papers, that dunce ought to be plucked. It was a humiliating circumstance, but I was compelled in honour to confess to that examiner, in private, how the thing had occurred. My next neighbour in the Senate House had been in difficulties about that very word, and had applied to me for assistance. 'My dear fellow,' I had frankly replied, 'I know nothing about it; I am not going to touch μέγας, but if you ask me my opinion about its declination, I should say it was μέγας, μέγασα, μέγαν.' I am glad to say this explanation saved the second-hand offender.

Notwithstanding this stupendous ignorance, I

F

suppose I had read more of one thing and another, when I left college, than most men of the same age, though apparently to little purpose. The nett results of a very expensive education were almost *nil*; a ten-pound note would have represented their value; and yet for the object I had in view, and which I afterwards pursued not without success, I venture to think that I by no means threw my time away. I had gained, for my years, a very sound knowledge of human nature, and made acquaintance with an immense mass of English literature of the lighter kind. Languages, living or dead, I could never acquire any more than music, for which I have no ear. I spent many years over French and German, but could never read, far less converse in, either language with facility. This unfortunate circumstance has enabled me to speak of translations with more familiarity and less contempt than is usual. It is generally observed, by those who can read foreign authors in the original, that 'everything is lost in translation.' This assertion, while undoubtedly a slap in the face, as it is intended to be, to the exclusively English reader, is not much of a compliment to the foreign author. It can hardly be denied that some works 'bear' translation; the Bible, for example (though this is by no means generally known), was not originally written in English. There are but few of us who have read ' Don Quixote ' in the original, and yet it is much admired. The fact is that some authors do lose everything in translation ; but some do not, and in some cases they retain a great deal.

Of ' Wallenstein ' it has been even said that the translator has excelled the author, though, if he did so, in my opinion he wasted his time.

The wits suffer the most (if one were to judge of Greek Wit, for example, by the volume lately published in English under that name, one would say, ' These are quotations from Mr. Merryman of the Circus '), and next to them the poets. Not ten per cent. of their original merit is left to them. But the ordinary prose writers, the historians, the essayists, and even the novelists, are recognisable enough in their new dress. Indeed, these last retain some very respectable attractions which it is mere affectation to deny them. Balzac, I admit, is not translatable, or when translated is not readable ; but Victor Hugo, even in foreign attire, is superior to most novelists in their native garb ; and the same may be said (at all events of his masterpiece, ' Monte Cristo ') of Dumas. It is undoubtedly a great deprivation to be near-sighted ; but it does not mend matters, and is also untrue, to say of such a person, 'he is stone blind.'

Soon after I took my degree I married. It was delicately said by a friend that, but for my intention so to do, I should have read for honours and distinguished myself; for what was the use of gaining a fellowship (and taking it away from some poor fellow who really wanted it) to lose it the next year or so by matrimony? Success, however (when I think of that μέγας business), seems hardly to have been a certainty, and it may be even thought by some people that I did not sacrifice much academical distinction on the altar.

I am only setting down some reminiscences more or less in connection with literature, so I say nothing about my marriage. If I were writing an autobiography, I should have to say a great deal about it, or else leave out the source and cause of the happiness of my life. I may remark, however, to those who propose to themselves a literary life, and can find a wife one-tenth as good as has fallen to my lot, that they had better make sure of her early ; for of a truth they will need a comforter. There is no calling, it is true, so bright and pleasant, so full of genial friendship, as well as of far-off but touching sympathies, so radiant with the glories of success ; but there is also no pursuit so doubtful, so full of risks, so subject to despondency and disappointments, so open to despair itself. It will not be denied that I have confessed to ignorance enough, but I know a few things well, and this is one of them. Oh! my young friend with a ' turn for literature,' think twice and thrice before committing yourself to it ; or you may bitterly regret to find yourself where that 'turn' may take you. Let every man be fully satisfied in his own mind, and have a reason for the faith that is in him. The calling (though by no means a phenomenal one, as it is the custom to assert) is an exceptional one, and even at the best you will have trials and troubles of which you dream not, and to which no other calling is exposed. I say again, verily you will need a comforter, and the best of comforters is she who sits by the hearth at home. Nevertheless, I need scarcely add, however confident you may be of winning your way to fame and fortune, be not so selfish as to link your fate with hers upon the prospects of an untried pen. For, if you do so, even though you should have genius, it will be the genius that is allied to madness.

One indirect but important advantage to a man of letters in early marriage is that, if a happy one,

it rescues him from Bohemianism.   It is a charming
'ism,' and he who has not a strain of it in his
character is to be pitied ; but it is *but* an 'ism '—
a branch of dissent, and not the Catholic and Universal Church of Humanity.

If one must needs belong to a sect, it is—for
him whose business it is to depict human nature—
as good as any, and better than most ; but it as
little represents the world as does the most conventional of 'genteel circles.'   The Bohemian writer,
who is called by the more charitable of square-toed
folks ' peculiar,' does not hold the mirror up to
nature much more than one of the genuine ' Peculiar People ' might do, if *he* should essay to repre-
sent it.   The Bohemian female writer in particular
—whose object seems to be to inform us that she
has never met a respectable specimen of her own
sex in her life—reflects for us the most distorted
images.

My first introduction, by-the-bye, to the Bohemians was very humorous ; and as the race—
except on paper—is fast dying out, it may be
thought worth while to mention it.   An eminent
member of the guild asked me to dine with him at
one of the old Legal ' Inns.'   I was very young,
and greatly flattered ; I thought I was about to

meet the most famous persons in the three king-
doms ; and though they were all of them of the
male sex, I felt it was incumbent on me to put on
evening attire. My host received me very cordially, but with a certain cock of his eye which I
did not like. He was in his dressing-gown and
slippers. My fellow-guests, eight in number, were
all in shooting-jackets. This made me a little un-
comfortable ; but they were very agreeable, clever
fellows, and we all sat down to dinner in the
highest spirits ; no, not all, there had been ten,
there were now nine of us.

'What the deuce has become of A. ?' inquired
our host.

'Oh, he has taken himself off,' explained one of
the party, looking hard at my shirt-studs ; 'he said
he would be hanged if he sat down to dinner with
a man who dressed in evening clothes.'

My position was exactly the reverse of that of
the guest who came to the marriage feast without
an appropriate garment: I was too magnificent
for the occasion ; but it was the very last time
anyone has had to complain of me in that respect.

All these things are changed ; the Bohemians
of to-day now wear purple and fine linen on all
occasions without the slightest provocation, and

when even the Rabelais Club dine together, it is, I understand, *de rigueur* to wear evening clothes, though I doubt whether 'the Master' would have quite approved of it.

My literary gains for the first year of my married life were exactly thirty-two pounds fifteen shillings; upon which, if I had had to live, it would have been cultivating literature upon oatmeal, indeed, and very little of it; but the next year my income was quadrupled, and from that time increased, not indeed by arithmetical progression, but certainly in a very unlooked-for and satisfactory proportion. It was at first mainly drawn from 'Household Words' and 'Chambers's Journal,' from the conductors of which I began to receive great encouragement. In the former periodical I had often two contributions in one weekly number, and I remember one occasion when there were even three. For the latter I wrote almost every week. Its editor was at that time Leitch Ritchie, a man of somewhat severe culture and fastidious taste, but of a most kindly nature. He welcomed fun in any shape, even at his own expense; it is well known that Leitch the painter was called 'Leitch with the itch,' to distinguish him from Leech the *Punch* artist; and one person (but not a

Scotch person) was so rude as to say of Leitch
Ritchie that 'he had the national complaint twice
in his name.' Even this he bore very good-
humouredly. He was in ill health, and endured
such suffering as might well have excused some
impatience with his contributors, but he took the
greatest pains with them. Even the rejected ones
(and this is perhaps the greatest triumph to which
courtesy can attain) had a good word for him;
while those who had merit never failed to find it
recognised. He made many a young heart to
rejoice in his time, but never more so than when
he wrote to ask me to come up to Edinburgh and
share his literary duties as editor of 'Chambers's
Journal.' 'I have long felt the need of help,' he
said; 'will you come and be my *co*-editor?' I
suppose five men out of six would have written
sub-editor; but the natural graciousness of his disposition caused him to italicise the *co*.

CHAPTER III.

MISS MITFORD.

I MUST now make a digression, or rather an interpolation, to introduce two eminent literary personages, to whom I owe a great deal, but the world much more.   My introduction to them took place before I went to college, but mention of them has necessarily been postponed, so as not to interfere with the natural sequence of matters.

A desk lies before me, of plain make, but mighty size : one that used to hold all sorts of things, from caterpillars (which never spun a thread) to 'cribs,' when I was a boy at school ; but which, for more than a quarter of a century, has held, 'those dead leaves which keep their green, the noble letters of the dead.'   Their writers were no ordinary men and women ; they have all left name and fame behind them ; but that which smells sweeter to me and blossoms in their dust, is their unfailing kindness.   It is not because they are dead

and gone that I feel so sure of this. With me
Death has never afforded, as it does with so many
folks, a cheap asylum for unpleasant people : I
think none the better of them for having gone,
though I am sincerely glad they went, for I am
sure they would not have gone could they have
helped it. But when I think of these my Mentors
(which most of them were), my heart brims full of
gracious memories. I contrast their behaviour to
the Young and Struggling with the harshness of
the Lawyer, the hardness of the Man of Business,
the contempt of the Man of the World, and am
proud to belong to their calling.

There are intelligent persons who make a living
out of their fellow-creatures by pretending to read
character in handwriting. It would be rather hard
upon their art to send them half a dozen letters out
of this desk. What would they make, I wonder,
for example, out of this delicate microscopic
writing, looking as if it were done with a stylus,
and without blot or flaw ? The paper is all odds
and ends, and not a scrap of it but is covered and
crossed. The very flaps of the envelopes, and
even the outsides of them, have their message.
The reason of this is, that the writer, a lady, had
lived in a time when postage was very dear ; like

Southey, she used to boast that she could send more for her money by post than any one else; and when the necessity no longer existed, the custom remained.

How, at her age, her eyes could read what she herself had written, used to puzzle me. She was known to those of the last generation as having written the most graphic and wholesome description of country life of her time; she was known to their fathers as a writer of historical plays which were performed at the two great national theatres with marked success—two of them, I believe, at the same time. Conceive what a fuss would be made nowadays about any woman in an obscure country village whose dramas were being played by the first actors of the day (Young and Macready were her exponents) at Drury Lane and Covent Garden! Yet this was the case with Mary Russell Mitford.

'My "Rienzi,"' she says in a letter now before me, 'ran a hundred nights in the best days of the drama.' She used to tell a capital story anent this play, illustrative of the ignorance of great lawyers of matters outside their own profession. One of her Majesty's judges was calling on her in her village home, and congratulated her upon the per-

formance of her 'Rienzi,' which he had just been
to see. 'It's an admirable play,' he said. 'Has it
any foundation in fact?' 'Well, of course; you
have surely read of Rienzi? It's all in Gibbon
yonder,' and she pointed to that author's works
upon her crowded bookshelves. 'Is it, indeed?' he
answered; 'then I should like to read about him.'
And he took away the *first volume.*

To hear her narrate that story was as good as
any play. I seem to see the dear little old lady
now, looking like a venerable fairy, with bright
sparkling eyes, a clear, incisive voice, and a laugh
that carried you away with it. I never saw a
woman with such an enjoyment of—I was about to
say a joke, but the word is too coarse for her—of a
pleasantry. She was the warmest of friends, and
with all her love of fun never alluded to their
weaknesses. For Talfourd (who, we may be sure,
did know about 'Rienzi') she had a very affectionate regard. I once told her what was at that
time a new story about his 'Ion; a Tragedy.' He
was very vain of that drama, and never missed an
opportunity of seeing it acted, whether in town or
country. Some wit, who had this narrated to him
observed, 'But surely he does not go to see "Ion"
now that he has become a judge?'

How she laughed, and then how grave she looked! 'You would not have told me that story, I am sure, my dear,' she said, laying her hand upon my arm reprovingly, 'if you had known that Talfourd is a great friend of mine.'

She had a right to rebuke me, for there was half a century or so between our ages. I had been introduced to her when a very young man, and had sought her advice about literary matters, with the intention, as usual, of taking my own way at all events. I well remember our first interview. I expected to find the authoress of 'Our Village' in a most picturesque residence, overgrown with honeysuckle and roses, and set in an old-fashioned garden. Her little cottage at Swallowfield, near Reading, did not answer this picture at all. It was a cottage, but not a pretty one, placed where three roads met, with only a piece of green before it. But if the dwelling disappointed me, the owner did not. I was ushered up-stairs (for at that time, crippled by rheumatism, she was unable to leave her room) into a small apartment, lined with books from floor to ceiling, and fragrant with flowers; its tenant rose from her arm-chair with difficulty, but with a sunny smile and a charming manner bade me welcome.[1] My father had been an old friend of hers, and she spoke of my home and belongings as only a woman can speak of such things. Then we plunged *in medias res*—into men and books.

She seemed to me to have known everybody worth knowing, from the Duke of Wellington (her near neighbour) to the last new verse-maker, whom I had just superseded ; he had become the last but one. She talked like an angel, but her views upon poetry, as a calling in life, shocked me not a little. I was in love, of course, and she shocked me even more upon that subject. She said she preferred a

---

[1] In the desk above mentioned there is a letter of Charles Kingsley's which describes Miss Mitford very graphically as follows :—' I can never forget the little figure rolled up in two chairs in the little Swallowfield room, packed round with books up to the ceiling, on to the floor—the little figure with clothes on, of course, but of no recognised or recognisable pattern ; and somewhere out of the upper end of the heap, gleaming under a great deep globular brow, two such eyes as I never, perhaps, saw in any other English woman —though I believe she must have had French blood in her veins, to breed such eyes, and such a tongue, for the beautiful speech which came out of that ugly (it was that) face ; and the glitter and depth too of the eyes, like live coals—perfectly honest the while, both lips and eyes—these seemed to me to be attributes of the highest French—or rather Gallic—not of the highest English, woman. In any case, she was a triumph of mind over matter ; of spirit over flesh, which gave the lie to all Materialism, and puts Professor Bain out of court—at least out of court with those who use fair induction about the men and women whom they meet and know.'

marriage *de convenance* to a love match, because it
generally turned out better. 'This surprises you,'
she said smiling, 'but then I suppose I am the
least romantic person that ever wrote plays.'

She was much more proud of her plays (which
had even then been well-nigh forgotten) than of the
works by which she was so well known, and which
at that time brought people from the ends of the
earth to see her. I suppose she was one of the
earliest English authors who was 'interviewed' by
the Americans. She was far from democratic, but
always spoke of that nation with great respect.
What surprised me much more was her admiration
for Louis Napoleon, upon which point, as on many
others, we soon agreed to differ. She even approved
of the *coup d'état* ; concerning which she writes to
me a little apologetically, 'My enthusiasm is always
ready laid, you know, like a housemaid's fire :'
which was very true.

Nothing ever destroyed her faith in those she
loved. If I had not known all about him (from
my own folk of another generation who had known
him well), I should have thought her father had
been a patriot and a martyr. She spoke of him as
if there had never been such a father—which in a
sense was true. He had spent his wife's fortune,

and then another which had fallen in to him,
and then the 10,000*l.* which 'little Mary' herself
had got for him by hitting on the lucky number in
a lottery, and was rapidly getting through her own
modest earnings, in the same free-handed manner,
when good fortune removed him ; but she always
deemed it an irreparable loss.   'I used to contrive
to keep our house in order,' she would say speaking
of her literary gains, 'and a little pony carriage,
and my dear dear father.'   To my mind he seemed
like a Mr. Turveydrop, but he had really been a
most accomplished and agreeable person, though
with nothing sublime about him except his
selfishness.

She had the same exaggerated notions of the
virtues and talents of her friends (including myself),
nay, her sympathies extended even to *their* friends,
whom she did not know.   Of course she had her
prejudices by way of complement ; and when she
spoke of those who did not please her, her tongue
played about their reputations like sheet lightning
—for there was much more flash than fork in it.

Literature in those days monopolised its disciples much more than it does now, when 'cultured'.
persons of all kinds favour the world with their
lucubrations.   Miss Mitford lived and breathed and

G

moved in an atmosphere of books ; and when she was not writing books, she was writing about them.[1] There is hardly any work of merit of that time—I am speaking of thirty years ago—which she does not discuss in these letters, and always with a vehemence of feeling and expression as though it were a thing of life.   A bad book—I mean one with distinct faults of style or tone—made her as indignant as a bad man.   Her views in this respect were of immense service to me.   A young writer who has high spirits (and mine were mountains high in those days) is almost always flippant, and needs the pruning-knife. ' Be careful as to style,' she writes ; 'give as much character as you can, and as much *truth*, that being the foundation of all merit in literature and art.'

My earliest efforts in story-telling were of a very morbid character ; an undisciplined imagination, with ill-health to help it, caused me to dwell upon the eerie aspects of life.   She warned me against all such monopolising influences. ' Let me tell you what Charles Kingsley told me the first time we ever met.   He said that he had flung himself into a remote and bygone historical subject

---

[1] ' This is the twelfth letter I have written to-day,' she says on one occasion, apologising to me for a shorter epistle than usual.

("Hypatia") in order to escape from the too vivid
impressions of the social evils of England at the
present day. They pressed upon him, he said,
unceasingly and dangerously, and he felt he could
not get too soon out of their influence. Once
before he had been so carried away by the meta-
physics of the elder Coleridge (Derwent Coleridge
was his tutor), that he for some years read nothing
but science and natural history. So there *is* a fear.'

Her own mind was a most wholesome one.
She delighted in simple pleasures, kind natures,
and enthusiastic people ; her love for the country
approached idolatry.

'So you do not write out of doors ? I *do*—but
in a very anti-pastoral manner, sitting in a great
chair at a table. I am writing so at this moment
at a corner of the house under a beautiful acacia
tree with as many snowy tassels as leaves. It is
waving its world of fragrance over my head,
mingled with the orange-like odours of a syringa-
bush ; and there is a jar of pinks and roses on the
table. I have a love of sweet smells that amounts
to a passion. My chief reason, however, just now
for being here, is that it is a means of enjoying the
fresh air without fatigue. I am still unable to obtain it in any other way than this, and by being led

G 2

in the pony-chair most ignominiously at a foot's pace through the lanes.'

The smallest object in nature was not beneath her notice, and any occurrence of the simplest sort connected with natural beauty impressed itself on her mind. 'A night or two ago my maid K. (that initial, by which she is always called, stands for her very Scriptural but most unmusical name of Keren-happuch), while putting me to bed, burst into a series of exclamations which it was impossible to stop : her attention, however, was clearly fixed upon the candlestick, and, following her eyes, I saw what seemed a dusky caterpillar ; it moved, and then appeared the bright reflection of a tiny spot of greenish light, now increasing, now diminishing, according to the position of the insect. It was a glow-worm. Upon the table were two jars of flowers, and one of wild woodbine from the lane had only just been taken away. With one or other of those flowers it doubtless came. But was it not singular ? Extinguishing the candle, I sent the candlestick down to the little court in front of the house, where it was deposited upon the turf, and in ten minutes my visitor had crawled out upon the grass, where it will, I trust, live out its little life in peace. K., who has lived with me fifteen years (and whom you must learn to know and like), said, knowing how fond I used to be of these stars of the earth, that, " now I could not go to them, they came to me." '

She was exceedingly attached to this domestic, and had therefore, as usual, the highest admiration for her. ' K. is a great curiosity ; by far the cleverest woman in these parts, not in a literary way [this was not to disappoint me, who was all for literature], but in everything that is useful. She could make a court dress for a duchess, or cook a dinner for a Lord Mayor; but her principal talent is shown in managing everybody whom she comes near, especially her husband and myself. She keeps the money of both, and never allows either of us to spend sixpence without her knowledge, and is quite inflexible in case she happens to disapprove of the intended expenditure. You should see the manner in which she makes Sam reckon with her, and her contempt for all women who do not manage their husbands.'

This is surely a homely picture, very characteristic, and appropriate to the authoress of ' Our Village.' She detested everything affected and artificial, of course, and what she would have said of the æsthetic and classical writers of the present day who call our old acquaintances, in despite of custom, by new-fangled names (such as Kikero for Cicero), I tremble to think !

I suppose in my brand-new University ' culture,' I had found something amiss with the pronunciation of the names in one of her plays, for she writes : ' The false quantity in " Foscari " is derived from the Kembles : John Kemble, Mrs. Siddons, Charles Kemble (I don't know about Mrs. Fanny), all Anglicised proper names as Shakespeare did before them. Indeed it is the best way to avoid discrepancies, and I have always found the most accomplished persons doing it whenever they can, and eschewing foreign pronunciation as they eschew French phrases—one of those worst vulgarities that smack of Theodore Hook and the silver-fork school. Remember, too, that my play was written before the publication of Lord Byron's.'

What an impression of the lapse of time does that sentence give us ! Here is another. Speaking of Haydon, whose Life by Tom Taylor had just appeared, she says : ' When I and Wordsworth and Keats, and many others, my betters, first knew him, and were writing, as if in concert, sonnets to him,' &c.: it makes me feel a veteran, indeed, to remember that I once was intimate with a contemporary

of such writers. De Quincey, however, to whom
Miss Mitford was afterwards, as I have mentioned,
so good as to introduce me, though born in the
same year, was connected with a still earlier race
of literary giants.

Besides her general admiration for good books
of all sorts, Miss Mitford had an especial fondness
for those writers who had sung the beauties of the
neighbourhood in which she dwelt, or were otherwise connected with it. I believe she loved Gray
the better because Stoke Pogis was the churchyard
he immortalised; that Pope was dearer to her for
his lines on her beloved Windsor Forest; that her
favourite, Burke, had a greater attraction for her
from his having chosen Beaconsfield for his place
of retirement; and that she admired Milton, even
more than her fine taste inclined her to do, from
his having lived at Chalfont.

It was for this reason, perhaps, though he had
very real merits of his own, that Thomas Noel's
verses so delighted her. He was the only man of
letters whom at that time I knew, and all that I
could tell her about him was interesting to her. He
lived a very retired life in a secluded cottage at
Boyne Hill, near Maidenhead, where he cultivated
his garden and his muse. I believe he was related to

Lord Byron, a circumstance which, combined with certain 'peculiar views' (as they were then called) upon religious matters, caused him to be regarded somewhat askance by his more commonplace neighbours. There was a rumour—whether true or not, I cannot say—that on the death of a favourite child he preferred to bury it in his own grounds rather than in the churchyard, which disturbed the minds of the good folk in those parts not a little, and caused me, until I came to know him well, to feel a 'fearful joy' in his society.

He was a very dark, handsome man, of reserved demeanour, and, so far, might have sat for one of his relative's stagey heroes, but he was in reality of a most gracious nature. I have letters from him, written to me when quite a boy, of a very interesting kind. He lived more out of the world than even the little lady at Swallowfield, and quite as much in books. These, however, were of a less modern kind. I never knew a man so well acquainted with the Elizabethan dramatists, or who could quote from them so opportunely. From one of them, perhaps, he drew his inspiration for the somewhat old-fashioned inscription on the spring in his garden, but the lines have a freshness of their own :—

Toads, and newts, and snails, avaunt !
  Come not near, nor dwell,
Where the dapper Fairies haunt,
  By this crystal well.
But upon the moss-tufts damp
  In the summer night,
Let the glow-worm from her lamp
  Sprinkle starry light :
And the butterfly by day
Here her painted wings display ;
And the humming bee be heard,
And the pretty lady-bird,
Clad in scarlet dropt with jet,
Here her tiny footsteps set ;
And the russet-suited wren,
Ever skipping out of ken,
And, in gayer plumage vested,
His wee brother, golden-crested,
Plying each his busy bill,
Hither come, and peck at will ;
And the redbreast on the brink
Of this basin, perch and drink,
Elf-folk such in favour hold :—
And if aught of human mould,
Wending hitherward its way,
  Haply here awhile should linger,
Let it heed this rhymèd lay,
  Harmless keep both foot and finger
And propitious glances fling
On the smiling Fairy-Spring.

Thomas Noel's mind invested all the scenes about him—and indeed they were fair enough to evoke it—with its own poetry.   In the ' Recollections of a Literary Life ' Miss Mitford has devoted a chapter to him, but unfortunately these two friends on paper never met.   The one was too much of an invalid, the other of a recluse, to surmount even the few miles that lay between them.   They were both passionately attached to river scenery, and Noel's ' Thames Voyage ' was one of her favourite poems.   His description of the swan and her family used to strike her as very tender and graphic.

Lo ! a sailing swan, with a little fleet
   Of cygnets by her side,
Pushing her snowy bosom sweet
   Against the bubbling tide !

And see—was ever a lovelier sight ?
   One little bird afloat
On its mother's back, 'neath her wing so white !
   A beauteous living boat.

The threatful male, as he sails ahead
   Like a champion proud and brave,
Makes, with his ruffling plumes outspread,
   Fierce jerks along the wave.

He tramples the stream, as we pass him by,—
   In wrath from its surface springs,
And after our boat begins to fly
   With loudly flapping wings.

Thomas Noel's lines on 'Clifden Spring' should be known to every lover of the Thames; but they are not known. Poetry did not even bring him fame, though it was its own exceeding great reward.

   Rhyme-craft, many-hued mosaic
   Of the mind, which souls prosaic
   Sneer at in their cold conceit,
   Is it not a pastime sweet?
   Oh! what twirling of the brains!
   Painful pleasures! pleasing pains!
   Oh! what making, marring, mending!
   Patching, paring and perpending!
   Oh! what hope, and fear, and doubt,
   Putting in, and pulling out,
   Till a word is found to fit!
   Then what joy is like to it?

   Brother bards, and bardlings all,
   Ye, who up Parnassus crawl,
   Ye who, at a rate surprising,
   Set your brains teetotum-ising—
   Boldly I appeal to you;
   Say, is not my picture true?

> Ye, whom mammon-slaves deem daft,
> Have I slandered sweet rhyme-craft?

What Thomas Noel was known, far and wide, for, was his 'Pauper's Drive,' of which the second verse often rings in my memory.

> Oh, where are the mourners?   Alas ! there are none ;—
> He has left not a gap in the world now he's gone ;
> Not a tear in the eye of child, woman, or man :—
> To the grave with his carcase as fast as you can.
>   ' Rattle his bones over the stones ;
>   He's *only* a pauper, whom nobody owns !'

This poem, until Miss Mitford rescued it from the almost stillborn little volume of poems entitled 'Rymes and Roundelayes,' was always attributed to another Thomas—Thomas Hood.

It has been conjectured, from the extreme polish and attraction of her letters, that Miss Mitford wrote them with a view to their publication ; but this I am sure was not the case. She often described to different correspondents the same occurrence ; and indeed I think that very incident of the glow-worm, above mentioned, is narrated in another place. In her day, letter-writing was an art of itself, and literary folk, not being so continuously employed in their profession as they are

now, could afford to practise it. In the next
generation authors did not write long letters, very
seldom indeed wrote letters at all, with the exception of Charles Dickens, whose genius was so
superabundant that he gave of it in all kinds, and,
as it were, with both hands.

Miss Mitford herself never knew him ; ill health
and, I am sorry to add, poverty, kept her for many
years remote from society of all kinds, which was
another reason doubtless why she devoted herself
so much to letter-writing. She corresponded with
scores of persons whom she had never met face to
face. In this way she had very considerable influence in the world of letters, which was always at
the service of her friends. She was never tired of
thus furthering my own ends, even when she did
not quite approve of them. I have set down,
elsewhere, the admirable advice with which she
favoured me ; the endeavours she made to turn a
very young gentleman, of unsettled prospects and
feverish hopes, to embrace some calling less preca-
rious than that which (as poor Leitch Ritchie used
to say), ' I hate to hear called " Light Literature." '
Never had a Telemachus so wise and kind a
Mentor ; but it was all of no use. I made my own
bed, and have lain upon it ever since with tolerable

comfort. At last she gave it up, and helped me as I wanted to be helped, not with the apostle's luke-warm assent, 'You will have trouble, but I spare you,' but with the liveliest interest. 'I should like to spoil you, my dear, very much, if I had the means,' she writes ; 'as it is, I am like Ailie Din-mont, who, when accused of giving the children their own way, replied, 'Eh, puir things, I hae nothing else to gie 'em !''

I had been brought up in the country, without the least link to literature in any direction, and she gave me introductions to everybody I wanted to know. They were of immense advantage to me, but one of the greatest gratifications they afforded me was **that** through one of them I became the humble means of establishing friendly relations between her and another large-hearted woman of letters, of whom Miss Mitford had at that time an unfavourable opinion—Harriet Martineau.

At first she seems to have hesitated to put her-self in communication with her sister authoress. 'I never saw Miss Martineau but once in my life, and have not happened to know, or to care for, the same people. Moreover, dear friend, without being in the slightest degree bigoted or prudish, I have, to say the least, no sympathy with her. . . . The truth is, although a clever woman, there is nothing about her that tempts one into a forgetfulness of faults as in George Sand. She is not, to my fancy, a woman of genius; all her works are incomplete. Indeed, the only things of hers I ever liked were her political economy stories, which I used to read, skipping the political economy. Fifty years hence she will be heard of as one of the curiosities of our age, but she will not be read. This is my Harriet Martineau creed. Nevertheless, if you still wish an introduction, why, you have a thousand claims upon me, and at a word I will put my prejudices into my pocket, and send you the best I can concoct.'

In spite of this, I had the audacity to be importunate. I had a great desire to be acquainted with the authoress of 'Deerbrook,' and I was going up to Lakeland, where she lived. To my reiterated request, Miss Mitford, with her usual kindness and good nature, gave way at once.

'I cannot bear to think, my dear friend, that you should have such good reason to believe me what in reality I am not, a ferocious bigot or a starched prude; so I do what I ought to have done before, and send you a note to Miss Martineau, who is beyond all doubt a remarkable woman. I

have never read her History, and did not fancy her
novels, especially the one where she compares (?) her
black hero with Napoleon, and even accuses the
great Emperor of killing him by cold and starvation ; but I agree with you that her boys' stories
are charming—how could I ever forget them!—
while her papers on Deafness and Invalid Life are
full of thought and feeling.   I have, at all events,
now done my best for her in presenting to her a
very different sort of visitor from those who com-
monly present themselves at our doors with letters
of introduction.'

CHAPTER IV.

BYRON places the best part of human life as respects enjoyment at two-and-twenty; 'the myrtle and ivy of sweet two-and-twenty,' he says, ' are worth all your laurels, however so plenty,' and he is probably right. If one has meat and drink enough (which at that age is important), and our tailor's confidence in us is still fresh, that is indeed the palmy time with most of us. But young gentlemen with a turn for poetry (or what they confidently believe to be such) have a still better time than others at this happy epoch.

> Verse a breeze mid blossoms straying,
>   Where Hope clung feeding like a bee,
> Both were mine, life went a-maying
>   With Nature, Hope, and Poetry,
>   When I was young.

One need not be a Coleridge to appreciate the conditions of existence under such circumstances, and

II

I verily believe there was not a happier being upon
the earth's surface than I when I went up to Lakeland at two-and-twenty with the avowed intention
and malice prepense of writing my second volume
of poems. A humorous expedition enough as it
now appears to me, but then the kaleidoscope of
life has shifted a little. Of what rainbow hues was
it not then composed !

> There was a time when meadow, grove, and stream,
>> The earth, and every common sight
>>> To me did seem
>> Apparelled in celestial light ;

as to my betters. Moreover, they were not meadows
but mountains, not streams but fine tumbling becks,
which I had come to dwell amongst, and, being a
south-country lad, these noble aspects of nature in-
toxicated me. I think the first snow on the fell in
October is the most charming sight that can greet
the eye of a lowlander. I have seen it in many an
October since, but I am thankful to say it still stirs
in me something of the old delight—

> I see, I see, with joy I see,

albeit my soul is bowed beneath her

>> earthly freight,
>> And custom lies upon me with a weight
>> Heavy as frost and deep almost as life.

It was in the early autumn that I first visited Lakeland with fifty pounds in my purse, which my dear
mother had given me to make holiday with (as
though all life were not then a holiday!), and an
introduction to Miss Harriet Martineau, The Knoll,
Ambleside, from Mary Russell Mitford, in my
pocket.

I had read many of the former lady's books,
including a later one which was just then [1] making
no little noise in the world, to the great detriment
of her reputation among the orthodox; but I had
never seen even her portrait ; and, though very desirous of her acquaintance, I felt a little frightened
at her.

Though I was able to understand that the
authoress of 'Life in the Sick-room' must needs
have a loyal and gentle heart, whatever appearances
might be against her, I pictured to myself a tall
masculine woman (rather bony), with the air of a
lecturer ; and the portrait was about as much like
the original (i.e. differed from it *in toto*) as the
portraits of others evolved from our consciousness
generally are.

---

[1] I am almost sure that it was 'just then,' but I repeat once and
for all that my dates are not to be relied upon ; I only profess to give
my impressions, which, however, are distinctly marked enough.

On the morning after my arrival in Ambleside
I inquired the way to The Knoll, a charming cottage
on an eminence, but quite shut out from the road,
and looking on the Rothay valley, with Loughrigg
for a background. A residence, I thought, as I stood
within its pretty porch, much more fitted for a poet
than a political economist. The bell was answered
by a neat serving-maid, who, although by no means
beautiful, had her attractions for me, for she had
been the subject of certain scientific (mesmeric)
experiments which had aroused much discussion.

'Is Miss Martineau at home?' I asked.

'She is, sir,' said the maid. Fashionable tarra-
diddles were not permitted under that conscientious
roof; but, if ever a face said 'Not at home!' it
was the face of that domestic.

'The fact is, sir,' she continued, looking at my
card, and certainly drawing no exceptional deductions from its perusal, 'Miss Martineau never sees
visitors in the morning. She writes in her study
until dinner-time.'

I could not, in fact, have committed a greater
solecism had I called on the Archbishop of Canter-
bury on a Sunday during the hours of divine
service. I felt at once the full extent of my crime,
and with a stammered apology, and putting my

note of introduction into the maid's hand, I fled down the little carriage drive abashed. It was not, however, I must confess, without a sense of relief that I thus found my visit to one whom a leading organ of popular opinion had designated 'a female atheist of European reputation' postponed ; and when, just as I had reached the gate, the handmaiden came flying after me with 'My mistress will see you, sir,' I wished she had not been quite so light-footed. I knew of course that I was indebted for this unusual favour to some monstrous exaggeration of my merits contained in the letter I had brought from Swallowfield, which only made the matter much worse ; but there was nothing for it but to return with the mesmeric maid.

- In the porch stood Miss Martineau herself. A lady of middle height, 'inclined' as the novelists say 'to embonpoint,' with a smile on her kindly face and her trumpet at her ear. She was at that time, I suppose, about fifty years of age ; her brown hair had a little grey in it, and was arranged with peculiar flatness over a low but broad forehead. I don't think she could ever have been pretty, but her features were not uncomely, and their expression was gentle and motherly.

'I am so sorry, Miss Martineau,' I began : but
of course I might just as well have addressed the
scraper. However, she gathered from my face that
I was making an apology for my untimely visit.
'Don't say a word about it,' she said ; 'of course
you didn't know that I was engaged in the mornings. How should you ? A poet, Miss Mitford
tells me.'

And she held my hand and shook it with
genuine interest, but also with some amusement,
much as a visitor at the Zoological might feel on
being introduced to a new arrival 'born in the
gardens' of a rare and unusual type. I am sure
the notion of a young gentleman, not over-rich,
being about to pursue the Art of Poetry as a profession tickled her.

'You are in Lakeland all alone, it seems ; that
is a claim upon my hospitality—even in the morning—which cannot be resisted ; not to mention
Miss Mitford's pressing recommendation of you to
my care. She seems very fond of you.'

Then I told her how very kind my friend at
Swallowfield had been to me.

'I am glad to hear it,' she said, 'but it does not
at all astonish me. She must have a tender nature.
What strikes one about her as a writer is that one

likes her books so much more than one's judgment
approves of them.'

I could hardly help smiling when I called to
mind the mitigated admiration which the other
literary lady had, though in another way, expressed
of this one. I was not so foolish as to contend
about what was after all a matter of taste, but
confined myself to speaking of Miss Mitford's
personal qualities, mode of life, &c., which interested
my hostess very much. We were by this time in
her library (though indeed there were bookshelves
everywhere at The Knoll), the view from which
naturally extorted my admiration. 'Yes,' she
said, 'the look-out is charming; it is sometimes
indeed so beautiful that I scarcely dare withdraw
my eyes from it for fear it should melt.'

She said this with great enthusiasm and with
her face lit up with pleasure. 'My little home,'
she went on, 'is full of pleasant associations. It
was the dream of my life to build such a house in
such a place; Wordsworth greatly admired my
choice of situation—he suggested the motto " Light,
come, visit me " for my sun-dial yonder.' 'Then
you knew him ?' I said. It was a foolish question
to drop into an ear-trumpet, but it was the first instrument of the kind I had ever met with, and it

disconcerted me extremely ; her offering it to me
was like a churchwarden stopping with his collect-
ing plate in front of one at church, where one
would like to be generous in the face of the congre-
gation, but cannot find one's purse. Moreover, the
idea of knowing Wordsworth, for whom I had an
immense reverence, rather overpowered me ; it
seemed like having a personal acquaintance with
Milton.

'Why, yes, of course. He lived only a mile
away at Rydal, you know. He was good enough
to take an interest in me when I first came to live
here, and gave me ' (here she smiled) ' much excellent advice. He said that I must make up my
mind to be lionized. " People will come to see you,
though of course not so many as come to see *me*,
whether you will or no ; strangers, tourists, and all
sorts ; if they are such as you must entertain, give
them tea ; but if they want meat, let them go to the
inn." It was very wise and prudent advice, but
you shall take an early dinner with me to-day for
all that.'

I was delighted, of course ; I was not the least
afraid of my hostess by this time, but felt that I
was encroaching on her hours of work, and said so.

' It is true you have made me idle,' she said,

'but it is such a lovely morning that I forgive you. Let us come into the garden.' We went out accordingly. 'My friend Mr. Greg [1] says that when it is fine in the Lake country one should never work, but though there are so many wet days, I cannot afford to be idle.'

I praised the freshness of her little lawn.

'Yes,' she said, 'but you have no idea of the trouble it took me to get the turf. You would think, perhaps, with these green mountains so near, that it was a common commodity, but the fact is, where once it is taken away it never grows again; the place is left bare. I could get no turf, in fact, for love or money, and was at my wit's end for it, when a very curious circumstance happened. One morning I found a cartload of turf lying on the gravel yonder, where it had been pitchforked over the wall. A bit of paper was pinned to a slab of it, with these words written on it in a vile scrawl: "To Harriet Martineau from a lover of her Forest and Game Law tales——A poacher." [2] I dare say

---

[1] The author of the *Creed of Christendom*, then living at Bowness, on Lake Windermere.

[2] I subsequently heard that on the morning after the event in question, Miss Martineau went over to Fox Howe (the house Dr. Arnold had built under Loughrigg) to narrate the event. Archbishop Whately, who hated her, was a guest there at the time; he

it was stolen, but that dishonest tribute to my merits always gave me great pleasure.'

We continued our tour of her little territory, and inspected the stall-fed cows, which were themselves not unknown to fame, as having been subjected to the influences of mesmerism.

For my own part I have never believed in these marvels. I entertain a Philistine scepticism upon the subject of most 'isms,' and at that time was very much inclined to laugh at them in a disrespectful manner ; but I never laughed at Harriet Martineau, though often with her. There was a tender as well as earnest gravity about her when expressing her views that nipped ridicule in the bud. Her belief in spiritualism was indeed a severe trial to me, but as she took the epidemic in a very favourable form—'I believe in spiritualism,' she used to say, 'but not in the Spirits,' just as my other friend took her Political Economical tales without the political economy—so much of consent to it as arises from silence was possible for me to give. Unlike Miss Mitford, who, without altering her opinions one jot, was ready at once to agree to differ, Miss Martineau revelled in

did not join in the general admiration of the poacher's conduct; he only shook his head. Some one privately inquired of him whether he doubted the genuineness of the letter. 'Doubt it ? of course I doubt it ; the woman wrote it herself.'

argument, and from an early period of life I have had the prudence to abstain from argument with ladies of whatever rank, or age, or genius. Only once or twice in my long intimacy with the lady of The Knoll did I ever get into hot water with her. One occasion was very nearly fatal to me, when I made an unfortunate mistake, which, painful and embarrassing as it was to me at the time, I can never think of without half choking with laughter. In her study was the portrait of a scientific gentle-man she greatly honoured, but who in my humble judgment influenced her mind for evil, and injured her reputation as a writer and thinker exceedingly. She asked me one day of whom the picture (to me unknown) reminded me. It was a striking counte-nance enough, full of restrained enthusiasm : but as it happened I remembered no one like it. ' Look again,' she said, 'you surely must see the resem-blance.'

I hazarded ' Robespierre.'

It was most unfortunate, for as it turned out she saw a most striking likeness in the portrait to the founder of the Christian religion.

'That,' as Anthony Trollope says more than once in his autobiography, ' was a bad moment for me.'

A ludicrous incident fortunately happened, the

same day, which restored her good humour. I had
by that time got so well accustomed to her ear-
trumpet that I began to look upon it as a part of
herself. It was lying on the table a good distance
away from her, and, having some remark to make
to her, I inadvertently addressed it to the instrument
instead of her ear. Heavens, how we laughed ! She
had a very keen sense of fun, of which however
she was quite unconscious. I remember her pointing out to me a passage in some leading article in
the *Times* which amused her excessively. It was
upon the subject of protection, and the country
gentlemen were depicted as foreseeing the nation
dependent for its corn upon ' the Romans, the Co-
lossians, and the Thessalonians.' ' How I wish I
could write like that ! ' she said, ' but unhappily I
have no humour.' She could not create it indeed,
but she could appreciate it very fully.

No one who reads these recollections can be
more conscious than myself that they are very
rambling. I have already wandered a long way
from the day of my first introduction to The Knoll.
As it is difficult to 'get on ' with some people, to
make any way into their minds and hearts, so that
we remain as much outside them after a twelve
months' acquaintance as after the first twelve hours,

so there are others with whom intimacy comes on so soon that it is difficult to replace oneself in 'the first position' of acquaintance. This is one of the reasons why a diary is so indispensable to an auto-biography.

Among the many foolish things that the cuckoos of the human race repeat with the idea that it has the wisdom of a proverb, is the remark that before a traveller can describe a place to others he must have lived there and known it thoroughly, whereas the fact is just the reverse ; after a day or two, or even less, the first impressions (which are the very thing he wishes to convey) vanish from his mind. So it is with a new acquaintance when he becomes our friend : his salient points are lost through our becoming familiar with them. I feel this very much in describing Harriet Martineau, whose friendship I had the privilege to enjoy for twenty years. My general impression of her is very different, I find, from the particular impression which she left on others who only saw her once or twice.

For example, with respect to that ear-trumpet (which had a great public reputation in its time) I have heard stories from persons as eminent as its possessor herself, which, though humorous and interesting enough, seem to me without foundation. Her enemies looked upon it as a weapon of defence.

It was in fact literally used in that fashion on one occasion. A right of way was in dispute at one time through certain fields (a portion, I think, of Rydal Park) in the neighbourhood of Ambleside, and the owner closed them to the public. Miss Martineau, though a philanthropist on a large scale, could also (which is not so common with that class) pick up a pin for freedom's sake, and play the part of a village Hampden. When the rest of her neighbours shrank from this contest with the lord of the manor, she took up the cudgels for them, and 'the little tyrant of those fields withstood.' She alone, not indeed with ' bended bow and quiver full of arrows,' but with her ear-trumpet and umbrella, took her walk through the forbidden land as usual. Whereupon the wicked lord (so runs the story, though I never heard it from her own lips) put a young bull into the field. He attacked the trespasser, or at all events prepared to attack her, but the indomitable lady faced him and stood her ground. She was quite capable of it, for she had the courage of her opinions (which was saying a good deal), and at all events, whether from astonishment at her presumption, or terror of the ear-

trumpet (to which of course he had nothing to say),
the bull in the end withdrew his opposition (drew
in his horns) and suffered her to pursue her way in
peace.   I wish I could add that she had the good
fortune of another patriotic lady 'to take the tax
away,' but I am afraid the wicked lord succeeded
in his designs.   More than once, however, I have
had pointed out to me over the wall—for the bull
was still there—the little eminence wherefrom, with
no weapon but her ear-trumpet (for she had her
umbrella over her head all the time to keep the sun
off), this dauntless lady withstood the horrid foe.

A great philosopher (but who did not share her
tenets) used to insist upon it that Miss Martineau
could always hear when she liked, and only used
her trumpet when she wanted to hear ; whereas at
other times she laid it down as a protection against
argument.   Nothing could be more untrue, though
I admit that she had degrees of deafness ; it varied
with her general health.

Again the author of the ' Vestiges of Creation '
used to contend that Miss Martineau never wanted
her ear-trumpet at all, not because she could hear
without it, but because she did not care to hear
what anybody had to tell her.   He said to me
once, in his dry humorous way, ' Your friend Miss

Martineau has been giving me the address in town where she gets *all her ear-trumpets.* Why, good Heavens! what does she want of them ? Does she mean to say that she ever wore one ear-trumpet out in all her life in listening to what anybody had to say ? '

She was no doubt somewhat masterful in argument (which is probably all that he meant to imply), but I always found her very ready to listen, and especially to any tale of woe or hardship which it lay in her power to remedy. Her conversation indeed was by no means mono- logue, and rarely have I known a social companion more bright and cheery ; but her talk, when not engaged in argument, was, which is unusual in a woman, very anecdotal. She had known more interesting and eminent persons than most men, and certainly than any woman, of her time ; the immense range of her writings, political, religious, and social, had caused her to make acquaintance with people of the most different opinions and of all ranks, while amongst the large circle of her personal acquaintance, her motherly qualities, her gentleness, and (on delicate domestic questions) her good judgment, made her the confidant of many persons, especially young people, which enlarged her knowledge of human life to an extraordinary degree. I never knew a woman whose nature was more essentially womanly than that of Harriet Martineau, or one who was more misunderstood in that respect by the world at large. She had excellent friends in her neighbourhood (in particular the accomplished family at Fox Howe), but those who knew her by reputation were afraid of her. At that time, especially, she had fluttered the doves in the conventional cote by the publication of 'the Atkinson letters' very considerably, and I found myself looked upon with some disfavour as her constant visitor. She was supposed, I think, to be initiating me into the mysteries of Atheism : whereas, unless she was invited to do so, I never heard her utter one word to any human being with respect to her peculiar opinions. It was believed, however, that she was compassing sea and land for proselytes, and people were warned against her from the pulpit. There was even some correspondence in the local paper as to the impropriety of her being buried in the churchyard, which was, to say the least of it, premature.

' I suggest the quarry,' she once said to me with a humorous twinkle of her kind eyes ; 'but Mr. Atkinson says that I should spoil the quarry.'

She was too used to unpopularity to be disturbed by it, and cared more for what simple ignorant but honest folks said about her, than for what was printed by those who should have known better. 'When you have come to my time of life, and have obtained a reputation (as I hope you will),' she would say, 'you will know how little it matters.'

I have learnt that lesson by this time; but, ah me! what would I not give to have those halcyon days again, when 'the hebdomadal conferrors of Immortality,' as poor James White[1] used to call them, could make one wince in every nerve with an unfavourable critique!

The only personal reference to her in print, save her brother's well-known essay against her in the 'National Review,' that I ever knew to annoy Miss Martineau was an article in (I think) the 'Leader.' It appeared at all events in some periodical of the kind to which she had herself contributed papers (*Flash of Memory*, 'Yes; the "Letters from the Mountains" in the "Leader"'), and there was, therefore, something especially disloyal and ungraceful in its publication. It pointed

---

[1] The Rev. James White, author of *Nights at Mess*, *Landmarks of English History*, and of the *King of the Commons*, and other fine historical plays in which Phelps appeared with great success: the pleasantest parson that ever filled (or I should rather say avoided) a pulpit.

out that since she had declared her disbelief in a
future state her testimony would not be received in a
court of justice, and that consequently, if any burglar
broke into The Knoll, and maltreated her, he would
do so, so far as she was concerned, with impunity.

The article was no doubt written in the cause
of civil and religious liberty, and with a disregard
of personal considerations which, had they affected
the writer, would have been greatly to his credit ;
but under the circumstances it was brutal enough,
and Miss Martineau felt it deeply.

To my kind friend at The Knoll I was indebted not only for my introduction to Lakeland—
for in her company, as will be narrated, I explored
the whole of it—but even for the selection of a
lodging. She was as good an authority upon
small practical matters as though she had passed
her life in attending to domestic affairs. In her
youth she had been famous for her plain needle-
work, and made not only her own clothes, but even
her shoes ; and when from illness she had ceased
to write, she applied herself to Berlin-wool work, in
which she attained a great proficiency. She took
a great interest in things about her, knew something of all the lodgings in the neighbourhood, the
extent of their accommodation, which afforded the

best view, and in most cases even their terms. At that time tastes were more simple, and persons who, like Dr. Syntax, came in search of the picturesque, were content with cleanliness and homeliness. Nevertheless, the whole district even then laid itself out for 'the visitors.' The irruption of the cheap trippers which Wordsworth feared (though he did write ' The Excursion ') had not yet come, but in summer and autumn the district was thronged with strangers, who generally made a considerable stay in it. When any of these were clergymen, the local divines got them to preach for them, and I remember at Bowness Church a curious incident arising from this circumstance. There had been a good deal of dry weather in the south, and an Oxford man who occupied the pulpit began to read the prayer for rain, when the clerk pulled at the skirts of his surplice.

'You mustn't read that, sir,' he whispered ; 'we don't want it.'

'But it's a prayer for a good harvest, my man,' reasoned the minister.

'That's just it ; the visitors are our harvest, and we want none of your rain.'

I need not say that this occurrence amused Miss Martineau (who had her own views about the rainfall) not a little.

'As to lodgings,' she said, 'though I am sorry to send you so far afield, there is nothing more suitable for your purpose' (and I was sorry to see she smiled, for I knew that it was the idea of my coming to Lakeland to write poetry that was again tickling her; it seemed like opening a small coal-store in the heart of Newcastle) 'than the farmhouse at High Close. It is an out-of-the-way spot, but commands more charming views than any house save one[1] in Westmoreland.

Upon this spot has since been built a lordly pleasure-house, with grounds to match, but when I lodged there it was a very unambitious dwelling, with a noble sycamore for its sole garden ornament, and a bull that loved its shade, and made the composition of verses under it a most hazardous operation. The house was on the summit of Red Bank, between Grasmere and the Langdales, and in addition to the whole stretch of the latter valley with its well-known ' Pikes,' looked forth on Diana's looking-glass (as Loughrigg Tarn was then called) and Windermere. Many a time did Miss Martineau bring friends to see that view while I was there,

---

[1] She was always most precise and particular as to the facts within her personal knowledge. The exception she referred to was a certain house in Troutbeck, where the visitors were *not* its harvest, and where the principal windows looked point-blank into its farmyard.

and dilate on it to them with ever-fresh admiration;
but I am afraid I had very little to offer them in
the way of refreshment beyond what Wordsworth
had recommended. To herself, however, eating
and drinking mattered nothing; she had no sense
of taste whatever. 'Once,' she told me with a smile,
when I was expressing my pity for this deprivation
of hers, 'I tasted a leg of mutton, and it was
delicious. I was going out, as it happened, that
day, to dine with Mr. Marshal at Coniston, and I
am ashamed to say that I looked forward to the
pleasures of the table with considerable eagerness;
but nothing came of it, the gift was withdrawn as
suddenly as it came.' The sense of smell was also
denied her, as it was to Wordsworth; in his case,
too, curiously enough, it was vouchsafed to him,
she told me, upon one occasion only. 'He once
smelt a bean-field, and thought it heaven.'

It has often struck me that this deprivation of
the external senses (for she lost her hearing very
early) may have had considerable influence in forming Miss Martineau's mental characteristics; but if it
turned her attention to studies more or less abstruse,
and which are seldom pursued by those of her own
sex, it certainly never 'hardened' her. Her heart
was as kind and gentle as though the song of the

birds, and the sigh of the sea, had fallen not only upon open ears, but upon ears attuned to them, while her patience when conversation was going on about her in which she was so well fitted to join, but could not, was touching to witness.

She could never understand why deaf people should so often be considered morose and impatient, while those who were afflicted with blindness enjoy a reputation for the contrary virtues. An acquaintance of hers once explained it to her in a manner entirely satisfactory to himself. ' Blind people, my dear madam, being entirely dependent upon their fellow-creatures, are obliged for their own sakes to be always civil and agreeable to everybody.'

' I see,' she answered, withdrawing her trumpet from her ear (to show the conversation was closed) and pressing one tooth tightly on her lip, as her habit was when displeased ; ' a very charitable view.'

Once only did I ever see her exhibit any active indignation. It was soon after her translation of Comte appeared, all the proceeds of which—and, considering the nature of the work, they were considerable—she sent, by-the-bye, to that philosopher, whose affairs were at that time in a far from

flourishing condition. In proportion to her admiration of his theories, she despised those of the
metaphysicians who 'did not know what they
thought,' and at this inopportune epoch a metaphysician of celebrity happened to call upon her.
She asked him to luncheon, and in ignorance, I
believe, of his hostess having had anything to do
with Comte whatever, he blundered upon the
dangerous topic. I gave him a hint of his peril,
but it is very difficult to stop a metaphysician, or
perhaps I was beneath his notice. At all events, he
delivered quite a lecture against Comte and his
creed. When he had quite done, Miss Martineau
put this question to him with chilling gravity :

'Pray, sir, have you ever read Comte ?'

The wretched metaphysician changed colour,
and stammered out, 'Well, yes, at least I have
dipped into him.'

'Dipped into him !' exclaimed Miss Martineau,
with sublime contempt (which reminded me, nevertheless, of Mr. Swiveller's condemnation of the
practice of sipping beer). 'No, sir, you have only
dipped into some review of him. When you have
looked at that shelf yonder,' and she pointed with
her trumpet to the bookcase behind her, 'you may
then say, for the first time, that you have *seen*
Comte's works.'

I am obliged, for the most part, to tell what I remember of Miss Martineau in place of letting her speak for herself (which would be far better), for a certain reason. I have very many letters from her upon all sorts of subjects, written, as she spoke, with excessive frankness ; but she had a great dislike to the publication of her private correspondence. It is a great pity, for she discussed people and things that have an interest for everybody with a personal knowledge of them that is most unusual ; I regret this veto the more, since but for it I could cull many an extract illustrative of a side of her character the least understood and appreciated—namely, its tenderness and domesticity. A year after my first introduction to her I came to Ambleside a married man, and my first child was born there, in the winter. Her kindness to my wife and myself I shall never forget ; I went in and out of The Knoll as I pleased, like a cat which has a hole cut in the door for it ; and her library was not only placed entirely at my service while on the premises, but I was permitted to take home with me whatever books I wanted. In return, I had the pleasure of teaching her whist and cribbage, which she enjoyed excessively, though I am bound to say that at the former game she was not A 1, or rather ' Major A 1.' Like Metternich, she took to it too

late in life, but at cribbage she rivalled Sarah Battle.
A Mr. Shepherd, an excellent fellow, the Ambleside
doctor, was usually our fourth, and many a merry
evening have we passed together. I think I so far
undermined her principles, which were fixed against
gambling, as to induce her to play for penny points.

Miss Martineau was very fond of my dear wife,
and anxious that we should come and stay with
her, when the advent of the child was expected, so
that it should be born in her house. This, however, we did not do. She sent a message to our
cottage -that December, when the event took
place :—

' I send to the back door (for quiet's sake) for
a bulletin, and shall continue to do so instead of
coming, so long as quiet is necessary. Oh! your
news makes me so happy. Your little Christmas
rose! I am glad it was a clear, bright morning
when it began to blow! How happy your dear
wife must be—only not too happy to sleep, I hope.
My dear love to her the next time you see her [a
little hint of the necessity for rest]. Come here,
you know, as much as you like, and make any use
of me and mine.'

The child, who was named after her, she never
forgot, but for many years continued to write to her

upon her birthday in terms comprehensible to her small wits, and always sending her some book suited to her age. When we were moving south from Scotland, in thanking the child for a book-marker she had worked for her, she bids her never to forget Edinburgh, 'Arthur's Seat and the fair city,' nor her affectionate old friend, Harriet Martineau.

She could write thus to a child, though her hands were at that time full of work, and her heart of sorrow, for some one at the same date had failed, which deprived her of 'a great lump of her earnings,' which might well have depressed, or even embittered her.

As regards money matters, I suppose no woman in the world ever regarded them from the same point of view. It is well known that a pension was offered to her by three Prime Ministers in succession—Earl Grey, Lord John Russell, and Mr. Gladstone—which (like Cæsar) she 'did thrice refuse,' it being against her principles to burden the State with any such obligation. And yet she was entirely dependent upon that reed, the pen, for subsistence. She liked to have things neat and comely about her, but her tastes were simple; she loved the country and its homely ways. In writing about an early book of mine called ' Melibœus in London,' she speaks of town life being very 'dreary' to her, and of it being impossible for rural folk to be too thankful for their particular privilege ; and she expresses her opinion that the least desirable existence is that passed in a country town, by which both sorts of privileges are lost. It struck her as most curious that elderly and even sickly people go on craving for the same amusements they enjoyed when young and in health, and she instances an old lady far beyond seventy who could not remember anything for one hour and could hardly stand, who was expecting her full share of pleasure from the Exhibition.

This must have been of course in 1862. For many summers after my first acquaintance with Miss Martineau I always spent a month or two in her neighbourhood, as much from regard for her as from my love for Lakeland, and she became very intimate with me and mine. Nevertheless, owing to her keen intelligence, I found it difficult to realise her extreme deafness,[1] and used often to

---

[1] Our intercourse reminded me of Tennyson's lines, for

'Thought leapt out to wed with thought,
    Ere thought could wed itself with speech ; '

or of Pope's, from whom perhaps he unconsciously echoed the idea :

'When thought meets thought, ere from the lips it part.'

address her when she was not prepared for it. She never lost her sense of the absurdity of this practice, and I can see the laughter in her kind eyes now as she snatched up her trumpet. She loved a good-natured pleasantry even at her own expense. On one occasion when she was bewailing her disability for music, of which she had been so intensely fond, I reminded her that she was better provided for in that way than most people, having both a drum and a trumpet always in her ear ; and twenty years afterwards I note, in one of her letters, a pleasant allusion to this little joke.

The degree of deafness, as I have said, varied ; and she tried all sorts of remedies. No one who knew her would suspect her of anything 'fast' or unfeminine, but, under the advice of some scientific person or another, she tried smoking. I had the privilege of providing her privately with some very mild cigars, and many and many a summer night have we sat together for half an hour or so in her porch at The Knoll smoking.

If some of the good people, her neighbours, had known of *that*, it would, we agreed, have really given them something to talk about. She only tried this remedy, if I remember right, for a few months, but she fancied it had a beneficial effect upon her hearing. For my part, I enjoyed nothing so much as these evenings. It is my fixed opinion that the conversation of even a dullard is mitigated and rendered tolerable by tobacco—he can't talk long without letting his cigar out for one thing, and there is less temptation to him, when he has a cigar in his mouth, to talk at all, for another—while all that is thoughtful in a man is brought to the surface by that benign influence, and one hears him at his best.

I need not say, then, what a charming companion, under these favourable circumstances, was Harriet Martineau.

It was about this time, I think, that, chancing to be in London, she consulted Mr. Toynbee, the aurist, upon her ailment. He did her little or no good, but was very kind and gracious to her, which made a great impression upon her. She was so pleased indeed with the interest he had taken in her case, that she resolved to leave him, by testamentary bequest, her ears. She announced this intention in the presence of Mr. Shepherd, who, to my infinite amazement, observed, ' But, my dear madam, you can't do that : it will make your other legacy worthless.' The fact was, in the interests of science, Miss Martineau had already left her head to the Phrenological Society. I asked the doctor how he came to know that. 'Oh,' he said, 'she told me so herself; she has left ten pounds in her codicil to me for cutting it off.'

There was nothing of course improper in such a bequest, but it was certainly very unusual; and I never afterwards felt quite comfortable —even at cribbage—in the society of the testatrix and her doctor. I don't think I *could* play cribbage with a lady upon whom I had undertaken to perform such an operation, but then I am neither a philosopher nor a man of science. As it happened, the doctor died before his patient, who subsequently altered her intentions altogether. I never, at least, heard of their being carried out.

On the rare holidays in which she indulged herself, Miss Martineau delighted in little excursions, and especially in introducing her visitors to the beauties of her beloved Lakeland. With two of these, whom I will call Messrs. A. and B. (not so much from delicacy as because I have forgotten their names), I once went round the Langdales in her company, when rather a curious circumstance happened. The rain, as is not uncommon in that country, came on very heavily, and we had to close

the curtains of the car ; then, in default of anything better to do, she proposed that each should
write down on a piece of paper their favourite
incident in fiction.   I forgot those which she and
Mr. A. selected ; but my own choice was that scene
in 'Ivanhoe' where the disinherited knight enters
the lists of Ashby-de-la-Zouche : the challengers
have carried all before them, and the populace (who
hate them) good-naturedly recommend him to
touch the shield of Ralph de Vipont as 'he has
the less sure seat.'   Notwithstanding this warning,
he 'strikes with the sharp end of his spear [to show
that he means business] the shield of Brian de Bois
Guilbert till it rang again.'   Mr. B. selected the
selfsame incident, which we all thought not a little
surprising.

It was in the third or fourth summer of our
acquaintance that Miss Martineau undertook to
write her Guide to the Lake District : it was very
literally a labour of love, nor did the pleasure to be
derived from it come, I think, short of her expectations.   We made up a little party together, and
'did' the district (with which, however, we were
most of us already acquainted) in ten days or so.
Besides ourselves there were C. (a barrister) and
his wife, D., a clergyman, and E., a senior classic of

Cambridge; and very merry we all were. We journeyed in a sort of covered wagonnette, and sometimes over roads that were scarcely adapted for wagons. We were once caught in a mountain mist above the Duddon valley, and, after much wandering round and round, found ourselves in the same place from which we started. 'I wish we had brought a compass,' cried Miss Martineau, and, when somebody suggested that we had 'fetched' one, I never saw an elderly lady more moved to mirth.

The most humorous incident of this tour, however, was, by the nature of the case, outside her perceptions. We had put up for the night at a little inn at Strands, near Wastwater, where the accommodation was but scanty. On retiring to her couch, Mrs. C. became conscious of some evil odour. 'It is terrible to think of, John,' she said to her husband, 'and I am bound to say it *looks* clean enough, but *can* it be the bed?' And from the bed, though it was as white as snow, the smell certainly came. Though as a rule Mrs. C. objected to smoking, she adjured her husband to light his pipe and puff the smoke in all directions; but, as Mark Twain observes in a case not wholly dissimilar, this device only seemed to awaken the

K

smell's 'ambition;' it grew worse and worse, till it became unbearable. 'I'll go to Miss Martineau's room,' cried Mrs. C. in despair, 'and ask her whether she happens to have a bottle of scent.'

It was a proof of the utter disorganisation to which they had both arrived that she proceeded to do this; for how should a lady who had no sense of smell encumber herself with a scent-bottle? Moreover, though she knocked at Miss Martineau's door repeatedly, it was of course labour thrown away, since she couldn't hear her. Then Mr. C. went to D.'s room upon the same errand. He found him sitting up in bed with a silk nightcap on, sniffing as though he would sniff his head off.

'Do you smell anything?' inquired C. superfluously.

'I should think I did! I have a horrible suspicion it's the bed.'

The fact was that the beds, which were 'home-made,' had been stuffed with feathers, the quills of which had been insufficiently dried; they gave us a bad night, but formed a very mirthful topic the next day; indeed I don't think I ever laughed so much as upon that journey.

The economy with which the trip had been effected (for we had lived everywhere on the best) very much astonished Miss Martineau, who congratulated C. (who had ' financed ' us) upon his arrangements. 'I shall certainly go over the ground again,' she said, 'next summer.'

'I wouldn't do that if I were you,' said the man of law ; 'these things lose by repetition.'

'But the cost of the pleasure is so moderate,' she argued.

'Well, it mightn't be so cheap next time. I took care, you see, to let it leak out that you were on a professional tour, and I think it had an effect upon the charges.'

I had rarely seen Miss Martineau so indignant.

'Then you have spoilt a most important item of my book, sir.'

I had some difficulty in restoring peace between them ; for the man of law would argue that *he* had not been writing a guide-book, but financing the company ; and was bound to do it to the best of his ability, independent of all private considerations. I need hardly say that he has since risen to great eminence in his profession.

Under Miss Martineau's roof I met at various times many remarkable persons, with most of whom I have since been on more or less intimate terms ; to her I owe my first introduction to

Matthew Arnold—'looking,' as old Crabb Robinson described him at that time, 'disgustingly young and handsome.' He is happily still with us, but the world has lost his brother William, one of the kindliest and brightest of men. I had been delighted with his fine Indian novel, 'Oakfield,' but the expectations it had aroused were fully realised in him. His appearance even at that time suggested delicacy of constitution, but he was very active and energetic. I took one expedition with him in winter on foot through Borrowdale. We talked of everything, from politics to sonnets, and agreed on most, but differed very widely upon the merits of the monitorial system. I had been for some time at the Military Academy at Woolwich, where, at that date, the system (with 'corporals' in place of 'monitors') was in full flow, with far from beneficial results. My companion, on the other hand, had of course an hereditary respect for it. At the time in question some letters were appearing in a London newspaper upon the subject, with leading articles for commentaries, of which, as he knew, Miss Martineau was the writer. 'She knows nothing whatever about it,' he said.

'But, my dear fellow,' I argued, 'there are the letters.'

'It is my firm belief,' he answered, 'that she writes the letters too. You may smile,' he continued, 'but I assure you nothing is more common. It is a mere newspaper device for the dead season. No one who has ever been at a public school of any kind——'

'My dear Arnold,' I put in, 'it is I who wrote those letters.'

'Not really?'

'Yes, upon my honour.'

How we both roared with laughter! I doubt whether those eternal hills, at all events with their snow shrouds on them, had ever echoed such mirth.

It was to Harriet Martineau that I owed my first introduction to heavy metalled literature. She tells us in her autobiography that, with the exception of Mrs. Marsh's 'Two Old Men's Tales,' 'I have never once, so far as I remember, succeeded in getting a manuscript published for anybody. This has been a matter of great concern to me, but such is the fact. . . . I have striven hard on behalf of others, but without the slightest success.'

Notwithstanding this disclaimer, I cannot but think I was somewhat indebted to her for my appearance, at what was certainly an unusually early age, in the columns of the 'Westminster

Review.' The article was called ' Ballads of the People,' and I got twenty guineas for it, which seemed to me a princely remuneration.

There is a great deal of misconception as to what can be done for the literary neophyte, as I, alas! (since in an evil hour I wrote a certain paper upon the Literary Calling in the ' Nineteenth Century' Review), have good cause to know. Unless a young gentleman has a natural calling (not only a fancy, or even a taste) to the literary profession, 'not all the king's horses and all the king's men' can set him up in it. By some improper exertion of private friendship it is possible indeed he may get something into print, and that —the extreme limit of outside assistance—is necessarily the end of him. His hash is settled, and generally not without some *sauce piquante* of unfavourable criticism. But if a young fellow has genuine literary talent, there is no doubt that his success may be hastened by friendly hands ; even the praise of those who are well qualified to judge of such matters is of immense assistance to him. It is not so much the whip that makes the mare of literature to go, as the encouraging pat upon the back, nor is the sieve of corn held in front of the steed, who has once had his nose in it, without an exhilarating effect. Those twenty guineas, for example, from the 'Westminster,' at that time were to me as good as five hundred ten years afterwards. That they came to me so early was certainly owing, indirectly, to my old friend at Swallowfield, and I told her so by letter. She wrote back to me, racked by pain and exhausted by weakness, from what was fated to be her death-bed : 'Ah! I wish I could have done a ·twentieth part of the good I wish you.' And a few days afterwards she was at rest.

Little did I think that in a very brief time my other friend, and I may say Miss Mitford's also— for the two ladies had kept up a warm and kindly correspondence—was destined to receive her *Nunc dimittis*, not indeed, as it turned out, from life, but from the world in which she took so active a part. Miss Martineau had been ailing for some time, and on going to London for advice received the news that she was suffering from an incurable malady ; the sentence, in fact, was Death, and though it was deferred for many years, she never tasted of the old life again. She still continued to write for her newspaper (the 'Daily News '), but for nothing else. Her very last bit of authorship, she told me, was the article on ' Convict Life ' in the ' Edinburgh.'

Throughout the invalid existence which she was doomed henceforth to lead, she was resigned and cheerful ; not a word of complaint, though she suffered much pain, fell from her lips or from her pen ; but she never recovered her old spirits. Our simple junketings and merriment were over. Year after year I used to come to see her, and every time there was a distinct decay of strength. Her intelligence remained as keen as ever, and her interest in the affairs of the world from which she was cut off; but to me, with the remembrance of other days in my mind, those visits were very sad.

At first I was admitted at the same familiar door, on the same terms as usual ; then only an hour's interview was allowed by the doctor's orders ; then only half an hour. She wrote to me, however, though even letter-writing had become toilsome to her, pretty frequently. Her own increasing ailments were dismissed with a word or two ; but all that pertained to those she loved was interesting to her, even to quite trivial details.

' Love to Tiny [the worker of the book-marker so many years ago], and all of you, from your affectionate old friend,' were the last words I had from Harriet Martineau.

CHAPTER V.

THE BROTHERS CHAMBERS—ALEXANDER RUSSEL—DEAN RAMSAY—HILL BURTON—ALEXANDER SMITH—EDITORIAL EXPERIENCES.

WHEN I first went to Edinburgh, it had for years ceased to be 'the Modern Athens;' the exodus to London had set in; and men of letters no longer made it their residence by choice. There were many persons, however, still remaining who would certainly not be designated as 'local celebrities,' and who could not have been found in any provincial town. They were also of various types. Robert Chambers, and Alexander Smith; Aytoun, and MacCulloch; Russel (of the 'Scotsman'), and Dean Ramsay; Hill Burton, and Gerald Massey, could hardly have been said to run in couples, or to be tarred with the same literary brush. But these of course were exceptional people. Society in general seemed to the Southerner, like the whisky toddy which had such an inexplicable attraction for the natives, a little stiff. Leitch Ritchie had warned

me that I should find it so. Though a Scotchman
himself, he had, until within the last few years,
passed his life in England, and among folk the
reverse of 'square-toed ;' his nature was frank and
emotional ; his humour was delicate rather than
robust ; he had no sympathy with the national
observances and superstitions, and unjustly, though
under the circumstances not unnaturally, took the
formalism of his neighbours for hypocrisy. He
was a great admirer of Edinburgh, but it was of
the place rather than of the people. In looking
on the Castle, or the Calton Hill, or Arthur's Seat,
'all, all save the spirit of man is divine,' was his
favourite quotation. This was a misfortune on both
sides ; for all who knew him liked him.[1]   For my
part, some of the best friends I have are Scotchmen,
and it would be as ungrateful in me, as impertinent,
to say one word against them ; but, as a rule,
when they are in their own country they need not
culture indeed, but cultivation ; it is difficult to
make friends· with them off-hand ; they have no
demonstrativeness ; and one seems, as the agricultural gentleman said of claret, as a liquor, 'to get

[1] Even B.—I will call him B., for indeed he was busy enough,
though he made no honey—speaking to Thackeray of Leitch
Ritchie, admitted that he was 'a very gentlemanly man;' but
'How does B. *know*?' said Thackeray.

no forrarder with them,' even when you *are* getting
'forrarder.'   With Scotchmen out of Scotland
this is not the case, or not nearly so much the
case ; but when they are at home it is so.   They
are difficult of access, and not like those imprudent
damsels who are said to meet the other sex ' half-
way '!   This is no very serious defect, nor one to
be resented with such bitterness as Sydney Smith
has spoken of it ; but to a stranger in Edinburgh,
like myself, it was undoubtedly a drawback.

As to hospitality, there was nothing to complain
of in that respect, for Robert Chambers not only
opened his own doors to me at once, but introduced
me to his literary friends.   He had long known
me, of course, as a contributor to the ' Journal,'
though I had met him only once before under
Miss Martineau's roof.   His manner was dry, and
though his eye twinkled with humour, I did not
immediately recognise it as such.   It was, in fact,
the first acquaintance that I had made with a man
of his type, and he puzzled me.   I never fell into
the Englishman's error in connection with northern
' wut : ' of epigram and repartee the Scotch have
indeed very little ; they do not understand the use
of the rapier ; but their humour, generally grim as
that of the Americans (though not the least like

it), yet sometimes very good-natured, I did not fail to appreciate from the first. Robert Chambers's humour was of the good-natured sort. His nature was essentially 'good;' from the pleasure he took in the popularity of his friends, I used to call him 'the Well-wisher;' nor did he confine himself, as so many benevolent folks do, to wishing. I was intimately connected with him for twenty years, every one of which increased my regard for him, and when he died I lost one of the truest friends I ever had.

His manner, however, on first acquaintance, was somewhat solid and unsympathetic. He had a very striking face and figure, as well known in Edinburgh as St. Giles's Cathedral, but a stranger would have taken him for a divine, possibly even for one of the 'unco' guid.' In London his white tie, and grave demeanour, caused him to be always taken for a clergyman ; a very great mistake, which used to tickle him exceedingly. 'When I don't give a beggar the penny he solicits,' he used to say, ' he generally tells me after a few cursory remarks, that " the ministers are always the hardest." ' He could appreciate a joke even upon a subject so sacred as the ' Journal ' itself. Mrs. Beecher Stowe had been visiting Edinburgh, and had had some talk, he told me, with his brother William. She spoke of various periodicals, and presently remarked, in an off-hand manner, 'You publish a magazine yourself, don't you?' So might a visitor to Rome have observed to the Pope, 'You have a church here, have you not—St. Peter's or some such name?'

As these reminiscences only concern themselves with literature, there is no need, save in justice to another, to speak in them of William Chambers: he was in no sense a man of letters; his style was bald, and his ideas mere platitudes; but because he had started the 'Journal' it was difficult for him to understand that its subsequent and permanent success was owing to his brother. Being childless, and of great wealth, he was enabled to perform certain public acts, which cast Robert, who was weighted with a large family, comparatively into the shade. But there was really no comparison between them.

I know no man who did so much literary work of such various kinds, and upon the whole so well, as Robert Chambers. There is now no doubt—indeed it was always an open secret—that he wrote the famous 'Vestiges,' though, until the late disclosure of Mr. Ireland, I had conjectured

from the style that the book might have been
written in collaboration. His scientific and anti-
quarian works were numerous ; his essays of
themselves fill many volumes, and admirably reflect his character—humour mixed with common
sense.

He held two pews, each at different churches.
I asked him why he had them in duplicate.
' Because,' he replied, ' when I am not in the one,
it will always be concluded by the charitable that
I am in the other.'

My friends, his daughters, were very lively and
full of fun, and on one occasion, on their coming
back to Edinburgh from some stay in London,
their father was thus congratulated by an old
church-goer on their return :

' We were glad to see them back again,' he
said. ' Yours is such a merry pew.'

William was always talking of the poverty of
his youth, and hinting—very broadly—at the
genius which had raised him to eminence. He
was fond of holding forth upon the miseries of a
poor lad, who had had to ' thole ' and toil for his
livelihood, and had afterwards, by diligence and
merit, made a great figure in the world ; and the
peroration—for which everybody was quite pre-

pared (*i.e.* with their handkerchiefs, not at their
eyes, but stuffed in their mouths)—used to be
always '*I* was *that Boy.*'

All this was hateful to Robert, and gave him,
as well it might, extreme annoyance. I remember
being applied to by the proprietors of an American
magazine to write a sketch of the lives of the two
brothers, and applied to Robert for the materials.
He laid his hand upon my shoulder, and after expressing in the kindest manner his regret at being
obliged to refuse me any favour, declined to give
me his assistance. 'I am sick of the twice-told—
nay, of the two-hundred-times-told story,' he said ;
'apply to my brother William, and he will be delighted to tell you the whole truth about it—and
more. He will be sure to say that we came bare-
footed into Edinburgh ; whereas, as a matter of
fact, we came in the "Flea."'[1] It was very funny,
but also very pathetic, and I need scarcely say that
the article never was written.

To my thinking there is no example of the
undue influence of wealth in this country more
convincing than the manner in which a good, and
one may fairly say, a great man, like Robert

---

[1] The 'Flea' was the name of the coach which at that time ran
between Peebles and Edinburgh.

Chambers was dwarfed in the public eye beside his brother. When he died there was a paragraph or two in the papers commenting on the event ; while the decease of William was dwelt upon as a national calamity, though indeed no one went quite the length of saying that 'the gaiety of nations had been eclipsed ' by it.

It is five-and-twenty years since I lived in Edinburgh, and no doubt great changes have since taken place there in social matters ; but what struck a stranger most at that time was the extraordinary disregard of the precept that the Sabbath was made for man, and not man for the Sabbath. A man might do many things much worse and be regarded with much charity ; but if he broke the Sabbath no one had a good word to say for him. The only parallel to such a state of things occurs in a certain narrative of a pious stockbroker who about that time was taken by Italian brigands. They were thieves and murderers of the deepest dye, superstitious to the last degree, and speaking a language of which he understood nothing ; yet a great deal of his captivity was spent in the attempt to teach them to observe Sunday. He made no other missionary effort, but at that he worked away, until he was ransomed, with the greatest perseverance : and I have no doubt he was a native of Edinburgh.

About this period a majority in the House of Commons had been 'snatched' in a division against the Sunday post, which prevented the whole country from sending or receiving letters on the seventh day ; as no post went out from London on Sunday, and there was no telegraph, this made two consecutive days of failure of correspondence ; the inconvenience was insupportable, and after six weeks the old *régime* was again adopted, but there was not, and I believe there never had been, any Sunday post in Edinburgh. The only alleviation permitted was that for one half-hour on Sunday morning the Unregenerate were allowed to send for their letters to the General Post Office. The scene beggared description ; though I made an effort to describe it—not in the ' Journal ' of course, but in ' Household Words,' under the descriptive title of ' A Sabbath Morn.' Hundreds of men, women, and children crowded the Great Hall, calling out their names and addresses at the top of their voices, while the letters addressed to them were thrown at their heads by unwilling and scandalised officials. It was a Pandemonium which even the ' awakening ' sermons of the day could hardly rival in their descriptions of what was awaiting those who read their letters on a Sunday.

This open exhibition of the Sabbatarian yoke was nothing, however, as compared with its secret and unacknowledged sway. In the street where I first resided, it struck me that, to judge by its drawn-down blinds, the people spent a good deal of their time upon the seventh day in bed ; on my second Sunday, however, I was undeceived, for my land-lady came up, and informed me that, though she had not spoken of it last Sunday, she must now draw my attention to the fact that it was not usual in Edinburgh to draw up the window-blinds on the Sabbath, and that the neighbours had begun to remark upon the 'unlawful' appearance of her establishment, which had heretofore been a God-fearing house.

What astonished me even more than this example of fetish-worship itself, was that I found persons, otherwise sensible enough, to endorse, or at all events to excuse it. Hill Burton, for instance, a man of exceptional intelligence, to whom I expressed my sentiments upon the sub-ject pretty strongly, replied that a 'national pre-judice was always worthy of respect,' or something to that amazing effect. An Englishman will listen

unmoved, and even amused, to a description of the
weaknesses of his fellow-countrymen, but a Scotchman, like the Greenwich pensioner of old, who
would never allow ' the Hospital ' to be found fault
with except by himself, resents it.

This was the case even with so robust a man
as Alexander Russel, of the ' Scotsman ; ' a great
personage in those days in Edinburgh, and far
beyond it. I remember saying something about
the stiffness of social life in Edinburgh in his
presence, and instantly apologising for it in rather
a maladroit manner. ' You have so little of it
yourself,' I said, ' that I quite forgot you were a
Scotchman at all.' ' Sir,' he said, ' I want no
compliment at the expense of my country.' When
I ventured to reply, however, that he ought to
accept it as being, probably, the very first thing
that ever had been done at the expense of his
country, his sense of humour at once came to the
rescue, and we became great friends. He even
stood a sly reference to the fact that no return
tickets were at that time issued from Edinburgh to
London, but only the other way.

I have never met a man with a keener sense of
drollery than Alexander Russel : and in his hands
it became a powerful engine. Readers looked for

his articles in the 'Scotsman' with expectations altogether different from those which the ordinary leader-writer awakens. They were not only logical and convincing, but had a strain of good-natured irony running through them which—save to the subjects of their satire—was universally acceptable. His anecdotes were admirable, and those who figured in them were drawn from the life. He used to call me 'that interloping Englishman,' and would expatiate with great humour upon the unnatural and unparalleled condition of affairs which had brought one of my countrymen up to Scotland to take the bread out of native mouths. We soon grew to be so intimate that he would joke—and by no means 'with difficulty'—upon the national peculiarities in my presence, just as though I had not been 'an interloper.'

Besides the humour of his stories there was almost always some graphic illustration of character in them. In Sutherlandshire and some other northern counties of Scotland, the Church was at that time ruled by certain elders of a Puritanic sort, but who had also an eye to the main chance. A young man in whom they were interested came down to practise the law in Edinburgh, and after a month or two one of the elders followed him and inquired of Russel how their young friend S. was getting on. 'I think,' he said, 'he will succeed, for he is a truly moral man!'

'He's well enough,' returned Russel rather contemptuously; 'but as for his morality, I am not aware, though he does come from your part of the country, that he is more moral than other people.'

'Hoot, man!' was the unexpected rejoinder; 'I dinna mean drink and the lasses, but gambling and sic things as you lose money by!'

A still more characteristic story of his was in connection with his own affairs. The Liberal party in Scotland, who were under great obligations to him for his advocacy as a journalist, had subscribed very handsomely to present him with a testimonial in hard cash. He was not a rich man, but he had doubts as to whether he should accept a gift which might destroy or weaken his prestige; and he consulted a fellow-countryman upon the point. The advice, as he told it me with infinite relish, was as follows:—

'If it is five thousand pounds, my man, tak' it; if it's less than five thousand, don't tak' it; *and say you wouldn't have taken it if it had been fifty thousand!*'

Unfortunately, from my inability, already alluded to, to master, or even to imitate, an alien tongue, I am obliged to relate these things in English, whereby I am conscious they lose much in the telling. As Russel delivered them, with appropriate expression and 'mouthing out his hollow o's and a's,' they were infinitely more diverting.

The former editor of the 'Scotsman,' when he retired to enjoy his well-earned leisure, was so good as to give Russel some particular advice. 'The conduct of a newspaper,' he said, 'is always a very serious thing, full of dangers and difficulties ; but in addition to its usual anxieties *you*, my friend, will every night have to keep the most vigilant watch lest that man Hill Burton should contrive to insert his theory about Scotch cheeses into your columns.'

It is not necessary to particularise what it was ; it will suffice to say that this theory—based upon the exposure of Scotch cheeses in front of the shops, and the treatment to which they were consequently exposed—was not complimentary or likely to recommend them to the purchaser. 'Day and night,' said Russel, 'for fifteen years, I never forgot my predecessor's warning ; a hundred times that theory endeavoured to gain admittance into

my columns, and by most unlooked-for channels ;
sometimes it lurked concealed in an article upon
the Crimean War, sometimes in one on the Divorce
Laws, sometimes in one on the divisions of the
Free Church of Scotland, or even on the Disrup-
tion itself : but it was always detected and struck
out. It was a duel to the death ; for I knew that
Hill Burton would never relax his efforts to get his
views upon Scotch cheeses into print while there
was breath in his body. On the morning of the
last day of the fifteenth year, he ran into my office,
waving a paper in his hand, and crying out, " It's
in, it's in ! "

' " What," cried I, " you persevering devil, not in
the ' Scotsman ' surely ? "

' " No," said he, " in ' Chambers's Information for
the People.' "

' My relief of mind is not to be described, and
I must also confess (here Russel turned to me with
a chuckle) that it gave me no little satisfaction to
think that it was your friends the Chawmerses
after all who'd got it.'

Russel was not a Radical, far from it ; indeed
he had that somewhat exaggerated respect for
hereditary rank which often accompanies Scotch
Liberalism ; but, apart from its political bearing, he

could see the absurdity of its claims as clearly as
any one. At that time there were two Lords of
Session in Edinburgh of similar sounding names,
Lord Neaves and Lord Deas. A young sprig of
the former's family once informed Russel that he
' belonged to the oldest house in England—Neaves
is in fact the elder branch of the house of Neville.'

' Dear me,' was the dry reply ; ' then in that
case, reasoning by analogy, Lord Deas may claim
a still more ancient origin.'

The wit and wisdom of Alexander Russel
would indeed fill a volume. Few men made a
more striking figure in local society than he did in
the times I speak of ; and albeit they were not the
great times of Edinburgh, he had many noteworthy contemporaries.

Dr. Simpson, though he was not then Sir
James, was at the summit of his reputation. His
appearance was remarkable ; Gerald Massey has
graphically described it in his dedication to one of
his poems, ' Body of Bacchus with the Head of
Jove.' Like many of his noble profession, he was
very generous, and always took into account the
means of those who consulted him. He was fond
of literature and literary men. I met him first at
the bedside of Leitch Ritchie, whom he attended

assiduously, notwithstanding the much more profit-
able patients that were always awaiting him. I
doubt indeed whether he ever took a guinea from
him. Simpson, too, was a great teller of stories,
of a different kind indeed from those of Russel,
but not less interesting, for the pages of human
life which lie open to the intelligent physician are
the most attractive of all reading. I remember no
one in his profession who more impressed me as
being a man of genius than he did. If not a wit
himself, he was, at all events on one occasion, the
cause of wit in another. He had, of course, an
immense practice in Edinburgh, but it seemed to
me a world too narrow for the exercise of his
powers, and I once inquired of a great English
doctor how it was that Simpson had never come
to London. 'My dear sir,' he replied with a dry
smile, 'he is quite right to stop where he is ; there
are no coroners' inquests in Scotland.' The Faculty
has a large collection of professional jokes, but few,
I think, better than this one.

Simpson had a warm admiration for the simplicity and tenderness of Leitch Ritchie's character, as indeed had everyone with whom he was
brought into close connection. He was one of the
last survivors of a school of literary men now

almost, if not quite extinct; it had the culture of
the silver-fork school without their affectation, and
the simplicity of the Bohemians without their dis-
reputableness. The author of 'Wearyfoot Common'
had been one of the hardest workers of his time;
'as a young husband,' he told me, 'I have often
written for the press for hours, while at the same
time my foot has rocked the cradle of a child!'
Composition—especially invention—under such
circumstances seemed to me to be an impossibility,
and I said so. 'Yet necessity, my young friend,'
was his half-grave, half-gay reply, 'is said to be the
mother of invention. You do not know what it is
to live by your pen *only*.' And indeed the difference between this and merely supplementing one's
income by one's pen is enormous.

In his time Leitch Ritchie had written upon
almost every subject under heaven. His total
ignorance of any matter was no obstacle to his
undertaking it; he cheerfully sat down to the task
of reading it up. To store the mind with general
information he held to be sheer extravagance; to
acquire what might never be wanted was a waste
of time, and he had no time to spare; it was only
rich men who could afford to fritter away their intelligence in that lavish way. On the other hand,

if he wanted to write upon a particular subject he would contrive to know more about it in twenty-four hours than any man of general information could possibly know. He was, as is well known, the companion of Turner in his Continental travels, and an authority on matters of art ; and he once wrote a pamphlet on the ear, for an aurist, which made that gentleman's professional reputation.

As an editor, this many-sidedness was of great advantage to him, and still more to his contri-butors ; scientific or poetic, imaginative or matter-of-fact, he could sympathise, more or less, with them all. It was a matter of boast with its pro-prietors that, during the long course which the 'Journal' had run, its contributors formed of them-selves a public ; and they were at least as various as they were numerous. I remember three re-markable contributions coming in one day, which my Co. tossed over to me, with a nod of introduc-tion in each case : 'That comes from an arch-bishop,' he said (naming him) ; 'that from a washerwoman, and that from a thief.'

Until a man becomes an editor he can never plumb the depths of literary human nature ; the position affords an opportunity for the most sur-prising studies, especially among the Rejected,

who form nineteen-twentieths of his constituency.
Vanity, as might be expected, is the leading feature
of this class; but the monsters it begets in the
way of suspicion and duplicity are almost incon-
ceivable.

It was by no means uncommon to find an
article, after the first few pages, gummed together;
the writer's notion being that his paper would go
through a very perfunctory examination indeed,
and that he would thus be in a position to prove
what insurmountable obstacles he had had to contend against; it never struck him that, even if his
device was not discovered, the first few pages would
have been amply sufficient data for his condemnation.

Others, however, would admit that their contributions were not uniformly admirable. 'After
the first ten chapters,' they would write, 'you will
find, Mr. Editor, that my story grows intensely
interesting.' When these precious MSS. came
back to hand, their proprietors were of course
positively convinced that the eleventh chapter had
never been reached, and so far at least they came
to a just conclusion.

Others, again, were really modest as to their
talents; they looked for acceptance on quite other

grounds than literary merit ; because they were only seventeen years of age, or because they were more than seventy ; because they had an aged aunt dependent on them for subsistence ; because their husband was a clergyman, and wanted his chancel repaired ; or because they were of Royal descent.

Some would-be contributors did not confine their efforts to 'make the thing that is not as the thing that is ' to story writing ; I am sorry to say they stooped to deception. Their articles, they would assure us, had been written with a view to our 'particular needs,' and 'had been sent to no other periodical ; ' which was not always true. We ' Wes ' have an almost infallible test for ascertaining whether our magazine is the first love of a con- tributor, and I have known language of virgin passion to be applied to us, after it had been addressed—in vain—to several other quarters. The most amazing of these hypocritical appeals were, however, personal, and directed to my coadjutor himself. The writers had known his works from their childhood ; had admired his genius from the first moment they had begun to appreciate literary excellence ; and held his name as a household word—yet never by any accident did they spell it right.

The discovery of these lapses from the path of
rectitude in persons of my own calling, or who, at
least, aspired to it, shocked me not a little.   It is a
comfort to reflect that I am narrating incidents of
a quarter of a century ago, since which (as is well
known) human nature has become another thing
altogether.   Moreover, if some of my editorial
experiences were disenchanting, there were many
more of quite an opposite nature, and which gave
great zest and interest to my new calling.   With
such an example of conscientiousness and good-will
as I had before me in Leitch Ritchie, it would have
been difficult indeed to take a cynical view of
things, even had I been so disposed ; unhappily I
was but a short time under his tutelage ; ill-health
compelled him to resign his duties and remove to
London, when our partnership (as he always called
it, though I was but *in statu pupillari*), had lasted
barely twelve months.

While I am upon the subject, I may mention
one or two cases—the individuals connected with
them being long dead and gone—illustrative of the
curiosities of editorship.   I had been in the habit
of receiving from a certain contributor some admirable sketches of low London life ; graphic, though
without offensive coarseness, they convinced the

reader of their absolute reality; and as the visiting
of the dens of the metropolis was not at that time
so fashionable an amusement as it as present, my
amateur explorer interested me very much.   It
struck me, I remember, that a large proportion of
the payment he received for his sketches must find
its way into the pockets of the policemen employed
as his bodyguard.

One day, after a long interval, he sent me a
paper called 'A Night in the Thames Tunnel;'
he described himself as being without the twopence
that ordinarily procured him a lodging, and as re-
sorting to the Tunnel—at that time a penny foot-
way—for warmth and shelter.   The same idea, he
said, had occurred to others; for on the occasion in
question he had found several homeless persons,
like himself, by no means of the lower classes,
huddled under the gas-lights, and waiting wearily
for the dawn.   The preface, as well as the article,
was so lifelike, that for the first time it occurred
to me that my contributor might really be as poor
as he professed to be.   I therefore wrote to ask
him if his affairs were indeed so unprosperous, and
making no apology if they were not so, since my
mistake was evidently, in that case, due to his
marvellous powers of description.   I got in reply

one of the saddest revelations I ever received ; it is sufficient here to say that my correspondent was utterly destitute.

That a man possessed of such talents should be in such extreme necessity seemed almost appalling. I went at once to Alexander Russel, whom I knew to be just then in want of literary assistance, and laid the case before him.

'Of course there is *something* wrong,' he said grimly : 'probably drink; but I'll give your *protégé* a trial.' And the Thames Tunneller came up to Edinburgh forthwith at a salary of 200*l*. a year.

The end of the story was almost as strange as its commencement ; my contributor (who did *not* drink, I am happy to say) kept his place for twelve months or so, and then departed elsewhere, when I lost sight of him altogether. I thought he had 'gone under' for good and all. Ten years afterwards a work on London life, purporting to be written by a Scripture Reader, made a great sensation. I read and admired it like the rest of the world, but my interest in it was vastly increased on receiving a presentation copy of the second edition, with ' my first success ' in a well-known handwriting on the title-page. It was the Thames Tunneller emerged to light for the second time.

There was a young poet among my contributors who also immensely interested me. His effusions were not only far above the average of magazine verse, but of great merit and still greater promise. He was not twenty-one, and yet there was nothing morbid in his compositions. They were so hopeful and wholesome, indeed, that it was impossible to have supposed, what was in fact the case, that he was suffering from an incurable disease and knew it. We corresponded pretty frequently. One day I received a reply from his father, instead of himself, announcing his son's death. It is too sacred to quote here, but what he said of the intense pleasure the young man had derived from the encouragement I had been able to afford him gave me a lasting satisfaction.

On addressing, on another occasion in the course of business, a pretty constant contributor, I found that she also—for it was a young lady—had passed into 'the sunless land.' In her case again the father wrote, but in utter ignorance that his daughter had ever been an authoress. 'The considerable sums,' he said, 'which she seemed to have at command for charitable purposes had for some time astonished us ; but her disposition was as reticent as it was benevolent, and she never let us into

M

her harmless secret.' The vanity which is supposed
to be almost inseparable from a young author's
character certainly did not exist in this case.

There were sadder incidents even than these.
Some one lost to his friends, or at all events to one
friend, either mother or lover, had written a poem
in the 'Journal,' which, meeting her eye long after
its publication, had apparently betrayed to her his
identity.

'I fear that what I am about to request,' she
wrote, 'is beyond your power to grant, but I
make it with an extreme yearning . . . . Can you,
will you tell me who wrote or sent to you the
lines entitled——? Was there a name or initials?
Was it sent from England or *Australia*? . . . .
Try, try, sir, to remember : a broken-hearted and
dying woman will ever bless you ! For pity's sake,
endeavour to satisfy me !'

Worse, though less pathetic cases than these
meet the editorial eye. The system of anonymous
publication is, in my opinion, far superior to that
of signed articles, if only for the reason that it
gives the unknown author his best chance ; but it
has, of course, its drawbacks, and one of them is
that it affords the opportunity for misrepresentation
and fraud. Mere vanity often induces weak natures

to lay claim to compositions which have attracted notice. I have known dozens of instances of it, some of which have had the most painful results. The lie once told requires a score of other lies to corroborate it, but detection in the end is certain.

'I hope I am not taking too great a liberty,' writes one unhappy father, 'in asking about an article written in your "Journal," of such and such a date' (let me once more say I am speaking of things that happened more than twenty years ago, and which can hardly therefore now offend any one). 'I have been told—and by himself—that it was written by a son of mine. I fear—I fear that vanity has induced him to tell us a falsehood. Will you be good enough to write the word "Yes," or the word "No" inside the enclosed stamped envelope?'

This young gentleman had only deceived his family, but there were some cases in which positive frauds were committed, and money taken for articles written by another hand. I remember a very well-informed individual doing me the honour of a personal visit and bringing with him an article on 'The Literature of Cuba,' in which island he described himself as being a resident. It was an interesting paper, and as I had never happened to near of Cuban literature, I accepted it. A few days afterwards he called again, announcing himself as being about to depart for his native isle, and inquired whether it would be convenient to let him have the payment for the paper in advance, a request which was at once complied with. When the paper appeared, months afterwards, I got one of those letters, half playful, half satirical, with which all editors are familiar, from 'A Constant Reader,' pointing out that it was advisable in a journal professing to publish only original articles to mention the fact when any exception was made, as in the case of the 'Literature of Cuba,' the whole of which, 'as you are doubtless aware,' said my correspondent, 'is copied *verbatim* and *literatim* from (I think) "Murray's Foreign and Colonial Library."'

This was reprehensible enough ; but not so bad as copying stories—of course not recent ones—out of other magazines, and not only getting money from us under false pretences, but embroiling us with our contemporaries, who in their turn borrowed with equal unconsciousness from us. One of them revenged itself by printing the name and address of the rascal, but the name was a false one, and the address he had changed. On one occasion a wretch sent us a story (of course, under another title) published twenty years before in the 'Journal' itself! This was seething a kid in its mother's milk indeed.

Serious as these fraudulent transactions were to ourselves, they were much more terrible to the relatives of the criminals, who were in most cases young people. 'I cannot conceive,' writes a father, ' what induced my unhappy son to take this course, as he did not require money, and his conduct in other respects has been most satisfactory. I have just learned from him the details of his misconduct towards you. . . . I beg to send you a cheque for the various amounts he has thus unworthily obtained from you, and earnestly hope you will see your way to accept it, without inflicting on him (and me) a public exposure.'

One of the characteristics of most young authors, or would-be authors, is their impatience ; they are in a great hurry to be accepted, and when they are accepted, they are in a still greater hurry to be printed. They have not the least idea of the exigencies of publication, and do not understand why their contribution which was sent in on the 20th of the month should not be in type upon the 27th. I had experienced this feeling of impatience myself, and had had cause to regret it. When I was a very tender stripling indeed—not more than

sixteen or seventeen at most—I had sent an article
to the 'People's Journal,' and received the joyful
tidings of its acceptance. It was the first paper
that I had ever had accepted, and I was wild with
triumph and delight. Rather to my annoyance,
however, when I purchased the next Saturday's
number, I did not find in it what I looked for.
However, I managed to exist for seven days longer
without bursting, bought the succeeding number
within the first hour of its appearance, tore it open
without waiting for a paper-knife—and was disappointed again. Then I wrote to the editor, very
calmly and dispassionately, pointing out that there
had been a mistake, and begging, in the most
courteous manner, that it might not occur again.
It did, however, occur again, whereupon I wrote
him another letter, not so dispassionate, and in
course of post received—most deservedly—my MS.
declined. With this recollection in my mind, I of
course felt no surprise at the impatience of contributors. The forms it took were, however, sometimes very peculiar. That the subject was as old
as the hills did not make the slightest difference.
The same anxiety for instant publication was mani-
fested for some essay upon the character of Queen
Cleopatra as though it were on a topic of the day ;

it never seemed to strike these writers that what the world had done without for a thousand years or so, it might still do without for another fortnight; they hoped to see their contribution towards the History of the Visigoths 'in our *next* issue,' with the word 'next' underlined.

One gentleman, who had sent us a pressing paper of this kind (I think on the Round Towers of Ireland), was especially unfortunate; he was an Irishman himself, he told us, which however was somewhat superfluous, for in his precipitancy he had omitted to give his address. A week afterwards he wrote in a great state of excitement to know why he had not heard from us, which nothing but the appearance of his Round Towers in print could, in his opinion, excuse; but in this case, too, he gave no clue, save the postmark, which was Dublin, to his private address. Then he wrote to say that flesh and blood could stand such neglect no longer, and that he was coming over to Edinburgh to demand a personal explanation; and still he omitted to say where he wrote from. Eventually he actually arrived, livid and foaming, and on being confronted with his headless correspondence, only burst into a roar of laughter, and observed that it was 'mighty queer.'

Strange as are the ways of the rejected contributor, they are not more peculiar than those of the voluntary correspondent. The interest he is so good as to take in a periodical is of course flattering to those who conduct it, but also involves some loss of time in the endeavour to satisfy his inquiries. Some are matter-of-fact beyond anything which the imagination can conceive. I remember publishing a romance of a certain island, not in the geographies, where things took place which do not happen every day, and arousing an unexpected desire in one of these gentry to visit it. 'I shall be obliged,' writes the intending emigrant, if you will kindly answer the following questions :—

'1. The date at which the account of this interesting spot was written.

'2. Under what Government it is placed.

'3. Price of land, and method of obtaining it.

'4. Language spoken.

'5. Average summer heat.

'6. Kind of sponge referred to ; honeycomb or cup.

'7. Occupations or trades most in request in the island.'

Another correspondent finds that a story, published in the 'Journal' some years ago, is founded upon a real incident in the life of his great-grandfather, and therefore demands that it be 'reprinted in an early number. Many friends would take a sufficient number of copies of the magazine to fully reimburse you for any expense ; and it would attract more attention if brought out in one of the numbers for this year.'

A good many of the casual correspondents of a periodical are evidently downright mad ; they use it as an escape-pipe for their lunacy, and thereby, no doubt, prevent themselves from 'jumping on their mothers,' or destroying their family at a blow : to extract their communications would be like quoting from a diary kept in Hanwell ; but the semi-sane ones are really noteworthy. These are generally scientific persons who differ from the usual deductions which science has drawn, and who have marvellous systems of their own, only awaiting development to revolutionise the face of civilization.

One of them had a 'mechanical hippogriff,' only requiring a little gas to inflate it, to go careering over the fields of space ; moreover (though, like 'the two little boys who only learn Latin' in the items required of a governess, 'it was scarcely worth while to put that in '), it had incidentally 'a method of expelling vitiated air by a succession of revolving fans, which, if thought advisable, *would discharge the whole atmosphere of one country into another.'*

Another of these quasi-scientific gentlemen was furious with us because we thought the world was round. 'I suppose, sir,' he writes, 'that there is no periodical in the kingdom which has done more to sustain the infidel imposture of the Newtonian theory than yours. Are you still determined to defend what you *know* to be the grossest fraud invented by man ? It is perfectly scandalous that a parcel of critics and editors should persist in fooling the public with the idea of a globulous world.'

The grounds upon which acceptance is demanded by the would-be contributor are most curious and unlooked for. One lady offers, in return for the satisfaction of seeing herself in print, 'to take in a dozen copies of your esteemed periodical ;' another, ' being the daughter of a colonel, has a large circle of friends who, in case of publication, would pur- chase the magazine ;' another has the literary re- commendation of 'one of the clergy.'

Now and then these applicants grew serious even to devoutness. 'Time,' observes one of them, ' is the gift of Heaven, not to be frittered away in the composition of mere medley rhymes,' but 'the torrent of imagination which impels her' can hardly fall short of positive inspiration ; if she is wrong, 'God forgive her waste of His precious time ;' if right, 'a post-office order will oblige.'

Some correspondents have grievances of the most unimaginable type. It occurs of course to more than one native of Erin that 'we have a settled purpose to caricature and misrepresent Irish characteristics,' otherwise in our Irish stories 'such mistakes would never be made in the brogue ;' but such complaints were sometimes not only national, but local. One writer inquires why the town of which she is an inhabitant is not represented in our columns by its local geniuses. 'I and a few other ladies,' says the writer, 'are desirous of informing you that this town is full of native talent. We have two poets of very high character and widespread fame—Mr. A. and Mr. B. —next Mr. C. ; and next Mr. D., and Mr. E. The first is a gentleman of fortune ; his poetry is a little strained, but very fine. There would be no chance of your getting anything from him, if (as I understand) you don't allow your contributors' names to be put to their productions. Mr. B. is one of our chief literary characters, a member of

several of the learned societies in London, and who
has published many things. Nothing could be had
from him upon the terms stated above. The next
is Mr. C., a tradesman, and a very fine pastoral and
descriptive poet ; Mr. D. is very fair, and has put
forth a book of verse ; Mr. E. is a wealthy retired
solicitor, out of whom there would be no chance of
getting any of his productions without money. . . .
I have no motive but your own good, and to show
how our city is neglected.'

I could tell stories without end of my editorial
experience, some humorous, some pathetic; but
the impersonality of the mysterious ' We ' ought, I
feel, to be respected. If the reader wishes for
more revelations of this description, I refer him to
the ' Editor's Tales ' of Anthony Trollope, which
are not only very charming in themselves, but unconsciously betray the kindness of heart of the
writer, and the tender conscientiousness with which
he discharged his trust. I may add, considering
the slenderness of his material, and the strong impression that each narrative produces on the mind,
that the volume is as convincing a proof of the
genius of the author as anything he ever wrote. I
once expressed this opinion to Trollope, who
assented to my view of the matter, but added,

with a grim smile, that he doubted whether anybody had ever read the book except myself, by
which of course he meant to imply that it had had
a very small circulation as compared with that of
his novels.

I have shown, I think, that the gravity of
Edinburgh life was greatly mitigated by humour,
but still it was very serious. Everybody must
remember Dean Ramsay's story of the dissipated
young man ' who went to too many funerals ; ' and
there was certainly something of austerity even in
its pleasures. With a large section of the community everything that had relation to pastime
was considered wicked ; and the booksellers they
patronised sold nothing but improving books.
Wishing to have some theoretical knowledge of
the national game, I ordered of one of them a
handbook of golf, and in due course received a neat
little volume entitled ' The Hand of Providence,
exemplified in the Life of John B. Gough ' (the
teetotaller). I took it complainingly to Robert
Chambers, who laughed till the tears ran down his
cheeks, and rather grudgingly observed, ' Now, why
should this have happened to you and not to me ?'

So seriously did society at large regard matters,
that the droller side of things escaped their obser-

vation.   A beggar man had stood on the old bridge for the last ten years with a placard on his breast, with this inscription :—‘ Blind from my birth ; I have seen better days : ’ and no one ever seemed to perceive that it was a contradiction in terms.

In Princes Street it was in contemplation (nay, for all I know it was done) to erect a marble cattle fountain with the motto :—‘ Water was not meant for man alone ; ’ but it utterly escaped public notice that such an inscription would be an encouragement to whisky-drinkers.

In my case, besides the general gravity of tone, there was an especial reason, which, in spite of the many attractions of Edinburgh, prevented my ever feeling quite at home there.   From native dulness —or to whatever other cause the inability to catch an alien tongue may be ascribed—I had always a difficulty in appreciating the niceties of language. The study of character—which is the only study I ever really cared for—was consequently debarred from me.   Many English authors have depicted Scotchmen in their own country ; Saxon chiels have gone amongst them making notes and after-wards printed them—though I don’t remember, by-the-bye, that the likeness has been ever acknow-ledged by the originals—but I felt that I had not their gift; that I could only see things skin deep. This annoyed me to an extent which to most persons would seem impossible and incomprehensible. I felt like a man seeking for gold, and who knows that it is beneath him in large quantities, but who has unfortunately neither spade nor pickaxe; I resented the mere roughness and nodosities of the ground.

What struck me as a curious feature of Edinburgh society was the extraordinary respect paid to professors of all sorts, though they were almost as numerous as colonels in the United States. In England we seldom speak of them (except in such cases as that of Professor Holloway) as professors, and still more rarely address them by that title, but in Edinburgh it was not so. I remember an amusing example of this. At a large party, at which Alexander Smith the poet (he had just been made Secretary to the University) was present, I happened to speak of him to our hostess.

'Notwithstanding all the praise that has been showered upon him,' I said, 'what a modest young fellow he is!'

She shook her head with gravity. 'I am sorry to say I cannot agree with you; for I have just heard him actually call Professor Soanso, Soanso, which I consider to be a great liberty in a person of his position.'

The notion of a poet being in an inferior position to a professor tickled me exceedingly, but it was not easy to find people to share the joke.

As a matter of fact, Alexander Smith was one of the most modest of men. The appearance of his 'Life Drama' had evoked a tumult of acclaim sufficient to have turned the heads of most men of his age; a pattern-drawer at some commercial house in Glasgow, he awoke one morning to find himself the most bepraised of poets; but it altered his simple character not one whit; and when the pendulum swung the other way, he took detraction with the same good-natured philosophy. 'At the worst,' he said, quoting from his own poem, 'it's only a ginger-beer bottle burst.' The epithet 'spasmodic,' so freely applied to him by the critics of the day, was singularly out of place; he was full of quiet common sense, mingled with a certain Lamb-like humour. In these respects, though of a widely different character, he resembled another Edinburgh notoriety of that day, the gentle and hospitable Dean Ramsay.

The simplicity of the latter's character extended

to his diction; in the last letter he wrote to me on quitting Edinburgh, he is so good as to say, after speaking of our intercourse, which was mutually agreeable, 'You are just the sort of person I find so pleasant,' and adds, 'Do you remember dining here with poor Aytoun? Something was wrong with him that night, and he was rather grumpy.' I am afraid he must have been *very* 'grumpy,' to cause the Dean to mention it; but it is only just to the reputation of the Professor as a good companion to add that I had no recollection of the circumstance.

The acquaintance of Dr. John Brown in Edinburgh I did not happen to make, and have always regretted the fact. He writes to me on the eve of my departure, *à propos* of a review I had written on his book 'Our Dogs,' in which I had termed him, to his great content, 'the Landseer of Literature:' 'You must let me thank you most cordially for your generous, pleasant, and altogether capital notice of "Our Dogs." It made me more than ever reproach myself for not having made your personal friendship. I have been cheated twice this week out of meeting you, once at Russel's, on Wednesday, and at Lancaster's to-morrow.' (Lancaster was a young advocate of great promise, of whom Dickens writes to me, from Edinburgh, long afterwards, 'He is the most able fellow I have met in these parts,' and whose early death was greatly deplored.) 'I shall watch your career through life with sincere interest, and if you get all that I wish you, you need not greatly grumble.'

If the prayer of a righteous man availeth much, the wish of so excellent a fellow as Dr. John Brown was surely not to be despised.

CHAPTER VI.

FIRST MEETING WITH DICKENS—CALVERLY—MY FIRST
BOOK—A LION TAMER.

IT was in 1856 that I first made the personal
acquaintance of Charles Dickens—a circumstance
which to me was an epoch in my existence. Like
all young persons devoted to literature, I had had
my idols. As a boy I used to have visions of un-
told wealth, with the power of laying it at the feet
of this or that writer, sometimes to be used for the
amelioration of the human race (I had often given
Thomas Carlyle a million or two, in trust, for that
purpose), and sometimes for their own benefit.
Tennyson I had thus enriched beyond the dreams
of avarice ; Browning I had made exceedingly
comfortable ; but the chief figure in my literary
Pantheon had been always Dickens.

For one thing (though that was not the chief
thing), he had given me more pleasure than any
writer—a circumstance which I have noticed often
arouses no personal gratitude : when a book pleases

N 2

ordinary folks, they no more think of the author than when a landscape pleases them they think of Him who made it; but with bookworms, even of the most superficial type, the heart warms to the man.

My late friend Calverly, the C.S.C. of ' Poems and Translations' and 'Fly Leaves,' when lecturer of Christ's College, issued a paper on ' Pickwick ' after the model of the usual classical examination papers, containing the most out-of-the-way details, and forming a crucial test of scholarship. He was so good as to oblige me with a copy of it, only a few weeks before his lamented and unexpected death, and gave me permission to make use of it in these Reminiscences. Little did I think at the time that he himself would find any place in them as one who had joined the majority. He was my junior by some years, so that I had not the privilege of knowing him at Cambridge, but in after years I often met him. We were neighbours at Grasmere for a whole summer, when I saw a great deal of him. His classical attainments were of course far beyond me, but not more so than his physical gifts. He was the best runner and jumper I ever knew; but my admiration never led me to imitate him. Nevertheless, in company with W. and S., his almost equally athletic friends, and himself, I was once persuaded to climb Scawfell from Wastwater. They went up it like mountain cats, while I (like panting Time) toiled after them in vain. 'The labour we delight in *physics* Payn,' was his appropriate quotation.

On another occasion S. and he were returning with me very late one night, on foot, from some 'sports' at Ambleside, where somebody, I am afraid, had entered himself as a competitor for the mile race as William Whewell, Trinity College, Cambridge, under which name he afterwards appeared among the winners in the local paper. It was exceedingly dark, and being very near-sighted I found it difficult to keep up with them, and was constantly denouncing them for the pace they put on. 'Now, S.,' cried Calverly (whose spirits were always those of a schoolboy), 'let us break away from this abusive miscreant, hide in the wood yonder, and pretend to be robbers.' And off they went. Their abominable intention was to ambush in the wooded pass between Rydal and Grasmere and jump out upon me where it was darkest. But though scant of wind I was not destitute of intelligence. I found, with difficulty, the short cut over the hill, by the Wishing Gate, which they had left out of their calculations, and, while they still lay in

the thicket bent on their nefarious scheme, their
proposed victim was at home in his bed.

Whenever I think of Calverly I think of fun
and good-fellowship ; of the 'wild joys of living ;
the leaping from rock up to rock ; the cool silver
shock of the plunge in the pool's living water ;' of
health and youth and strength.   Alas, alas !

Here are some extracts from the famous examination paper.

.Christ's College, Christmas, 1857.

THE POSTHUMOUS PAPERS OF THE PICKWICK CLUB.

1. Mention any occasions on which it is specified that the Fat
Boy was *not* asleep ; and that (1) Mr. Pickwick and (2) Mr.
Weller, senr., ran. · Deduce from expressions used on one occa-
sion Mr. Pickwick's maximum of speed.

3. Who were Mr. Staple, Goodwin, Mr. Brooks, Villam, Mrs.
Bunkin ; 'old Nobs,' 'cast-iron head,' 'young Bantam ? '

9. Describe the common Profeel-machine.

10. State the component parts of Dog's-nose ; and simplify the
expression ' taking a grinder.'

11. On finding his principal in the Pound, Mr. Weller and the
town-beadle varied directly.   Show that the latter was ultimately
eliminated, and state the number of rounds in the square which is
not described.

12. 'Anything for air and exercise; as the wery old donkey
observed ven they voke him up from his deathbed to carry ten
gen'lmen to Greenwich in a tax-cart.'   Illustrate this by stating any
remark recorded in the Pickwick papers to have been made by a
(previously) dumb animal, with the circumstances under which he
made it.

17. Give Weller's Theories for the Extraction of Mr. Pickwick
from the Fleet.   Where was his wife's will found ?

18. How did the old lady make memorandum, and of what, at whist? Shew that there were at least three times as many fiddles as harps in Muggleton at the time of the ball at Manor Farm.

23. 'She's a-swelling wisibly.' When did the same phenomenon occur again, and what fluid caused the pressure on the body in the latter case?

24. How did Mr. Weller, senior, define the Funds; and what view did he take of reduced Consols? In what terms is his elastic force described when he assaulted Mr. Stiggins at the Meeting? Write down the name of the Meeting.

25. 'προβατογνώμων: "A good judge of cattle; hence, a good judge of character."' Note on Æsch. Ag.—Illustrate the theory involved by a remark of the parent Weller.

30. Who, besides Mr. Pickwick, is recorded to have worn gaiters?

The prizes were a 'first edition' of 'Pickwick,' and it will be interesting to many to learn that the two prizemen were Walter Besant and Professor Skeat. If 'Pickwick' were to-day made a text-book for 'exams.' in general, the replies would no doubt be satisfactory, for there is now a concordance for the whole of Dickens; but in 1857 there was no need of cramming, for every one knew the book and quoted it. I have the vanity to believe, had I been qualified as a candidate, I should have gained a prize: at all events, I had my Dickens at my fingers' ends, and the notion of feeling him there in the flesh—of shaking hands with him—was positively intoxicating. He came to Edinburgh to give his public readings for the first time, and had little time to spare of course for private intercourse. On the evening after his arrival he was so good, however, as to propose a meeting.

'The hours and days,' he writes, 'run away, while I am thus occupied, so imperceptibly that I do nothing that I propose to myself to do. I thought we should have walked ten miles together by this time. To-morrow morning I am going to take my daughters out to Hawthornden, and it occurs to me to ask if you could spare time to go with us on the expedition.'

If I had had only twenty-four hours to live I should have 'spared time' for such a purpose, which did not indeed seem to trench upon my earthly span at all, but to be a foretaste of Paradise. Such enthusiasm is unknown in these days, wherein Dickens himself, as an American writer informs us, 'is no longer to be endured,'[1] and will doubtless excite some ridicule ; but for my part I am not one whit ashamed of it. Nay, contemptible as the confession may appear, I feel the same love and admiration for Charles Dickens now as I did then. What indeed astonished even me, I remember, at the

---

[1] The statement in a recent publication that 4,239,000 volumes of Dickens's works have been sold in England alone since his death, seems to be at variance with this gentleman's view.

time, was that personal acquaintance with him increased rather than diminished his marvellous attraction for me. In general society, especially if it has been of an artificial kind, I have known his manner to betray some sense of effort, but in a company with whom he could feel at home, I have never met a man more natural or more charming. He never wasted time in commonplaces—though a lively talker, he never uttered a platitude—and what he had to say he said as if he meant it. On an occasion, which many of my readers will call to mind, he once spoke of himself as 'very human:' he did so, of course, in a depreciatory sense; he was the last person in the world to affect to possess any other nature than that of his fellows. When some one said, 'How wicked the world is!' he answered, 'True; and what a satisfaction it is that neither you nor I belong to it!' But the fact is, it was this very humanity which was his charm. Whatever there was of him was real without padding; and whatever was genuine in others had a sympathetic attraction for him.

The subject, however, which most interested him (and, in a less degree, this was also the case with Thackeray) was the dramatic—nay, even the melodramatic—side of human nature. He had stories without end, taken from the very page of life, of quite a different kind from those with which he made his readers familiar. There are, indeed, indications of this tendency in his writings, as in the tales interspersed in ' Pickwick,' in the abandoned commencement of ' Humphrey's Clock, ' and more markedly, in his occasional sketches, but they were much more common in his private talk.

When visiting the exhibition of Hablot Browne's pictures the other day I was much struck by the fact that, when indulging his own taste, the subjects chosen by the artist were not humorous but sombre and eerie. This, I feel sure, was what made him so acceptable an illustrator to Dickens. He could not only depict humorous scenes with feeling, but also such grim imaginings as the old Roman looking down on dead Mr. Tulkinghorn, and the Ghost Walk at Chesney Wold. The mind of Dickens, which most of his readers picture to themselves as revelling in sunshine, was in fact more attracted to the darker side of life, though there was far too much of geniality in him to permit it to become morbid.

On the occasion of our first meeting, however, I saw nothing of all this : he was full of fun and brightness, and in five minutes I felt as much at my

case with him as though I had known him as long
as I had known his books. It was not one of the
days on which Hawthornden was open to the public,
and we had much difficulty in obtaining admittance
at the lodge ; and when we got to the house we
were detained there again, and there was a difficulty about seeing the glen. I went within doors
and expostulated, but for a long time without
success : the inmates, I am sorry to say, did not
seem to be acquainted with Dickens's name—a circumstance which, though it would only have made
him laugh the more, I did not venture to disclose.
The fancy picture which he drew of my detention
in that feudal abode, and of the mediæval tortures
which had probably been inflicted upon me, made
ample amends, however, for what I had suffered on
behalf of the party. In the end, we saw all that
was to be seen ; and never shall I forget the face
of the hereditary guide and gatekeeper when
Dickens tipped him in his usual lavish manner.

This retainer had not thought much of him
before—indeed, had obviously never heard of him
—but his salute at parting could not have been
more deferential had the author of ' Pickwick '
been the Lord of the Isles. The humours of the
day must have made some impression upon Dickens

himself, for in a letter two years afterwards he reminds me of the imprisonment I had suffered for
his sake in the gloomy cells of Hawthornden. Late
that night I supped with him—after his reading—
at his hotel, alone ; after which I discarded for ever
the picture which I had made in my mind of him,
and substituted for it a still pleasanter one, taken
from life.

In the following year I published my first book,
a collection of 'Stories and Sketches,' taken from
my contributions to 'Household Words' and
'Chambers's Journal.'   I have been often asked by
young authors whether 'it pays' to republish such
articles.   Directly, it certainly does not pay, for
the venture is almost always a pecuniary loss ; but
indirectly, if the articles are really good, it is very
remunerative.   It introduces the writer not only to
the public (who, of course, have hitherto never
heard of him), but to editors in general, who thus
obtain a good specimen of his powers.   In old
days this system of advertising one's literary
wares was not so common as at present : it was
generally resorted to only by geniuses in humble
life whose works were published by subscription ;
and whatever advantages they derived from the
system were more than counterbalanced by the

latter fact. One of them, who afterwards became very famous, observed to me that he had bought his first reputation at a much higher price than those who had paid for it—*i.e.* who had published at their own expense. 'Every one who subscribed five shillings to that book of mine is in a position to say that but for him I should never have been heard of; and about two out of three do say so.' But this is only to admit that the possession of spare cash in literature is as useful as it is in all other professions.

Before leaving this subject, I should add, for fear of being thought to recommend 'rushing into print,' that while many writers have been benefited by early publication, quite as many (even of those who have afterwards made their mark in the world) have lived to repent it. In youth—though I think this is not the case with us in maturity—we are not such good judges of our own work as other people; we are apt to make comparisons between it and that of other writers, instead of estimating its intrinsic worth, which alone ought to guide us.[1]

[1] A similar feeling causes some contributors to endeavour to recommend themselves to the notice of an editor in the following conciliatory manner : 'Without self-flattery, I think I may venture to say that the paper I send to you, however modest in merit, is at all events superior to the majority of the articles in your esteemed magazine.

My next book was a narrative of school and college life, called the 'Foster Brothers,' which had a very fair success, and was republished, as everything I subsequently wrote has been, in America. My works have also been translated into various languages. Perhaps nothing gives a young author so much pleasure as to see the product of his brain in a foreign tongue, even though (as in my case) he cannot read it. To the satisfaction I derived from the 'Foster Brothers' there was, however, a terrible drawback, in the form of a most scathing notice in the 'Saturday Review.' It was headed—on account of certain democratic opinions the volume had displayed—the 'Bloated Aristocracy,' and made me most thoroughly miserable. The writer, now one of her Majesty's judges, has laughed with me since about it, but I am never so tickled with the reminiscence as he is. I have a great personal regard for him, but note with pleasure that the newspapers describe him as 'a hanging judge.'

In acknowledging the receipt of this book in his usual kind and cordial manner, Dickens misspells it 'Forster Brothers,' and apologises for the mistake by saying 'this is because I am always thinking of my friend John Forster.' I afterwards received (as will be mentioned in its proper place) a still more curious proof of his devotion to one who, from many points of view, one would have judged to be little in sympathy with him.

By this time I had made some success as a writer of lively sketches and humorous articles ; rejection, so far as they were concerned, had become as rare with me as acceptance had formerly been ; and my aspirations began to be more ambitious. It struck me that I might one day write a successful novel. This is not quite so easy, however, as to express your opinion about a novel written by somebody else. The proper construction of such a work comes by experience, and never by intuition : when a young writer attempts it, he succeeds at best in writing a narrative and not a novel ; he takes a character, generally more or less like himself, and describes his career from the cradle to the altar, which he considers to be equivalent to the grave. It is, in fact, an autobiography of a person of whom no one has ever heard, and the only chance, therefore, for its success is that the incidents in the hero's life should be of a striking kind.

Fortune was so good as to favour me with quite a pattern hero for this purpose, in a gentleman who had achieved a reputation as a tamer of wild beasts. What his real name was I never knew, but his pro-

fessional one was, if not romantic, at least remarkable. It was Tickerocandua. I made his acquaintance when visiting a travelling menagerie of which
he was the pride and ornament, and we became very
friendly. His life up to the time he had entered
upon his present dangerous calling had been un-
eventful enough ; but I perceived in him the
materials of excellent 'copy.' I thought that he
would make a capital example of a family scapegrace, of pluck and spirit, who, more sinned against
than sinning, had run away from his friends and
taken to tiger-taming. On every 'lawful day,' as
the Scotch phrase runs, he was engaged with his
animals—witching the world with feats compared
with which the noblest horsemanship sank into
insignificance. So he came to supper with me on
a Sunday. Our little servant-maid's difficulty in
announcing him as ' Mr. Tickerocandua ' was considerable : and when he began to talk of his tooth-
and-claw experiences, I thought her eyes would
have come out of her head. He was the politest
person I ever met with, for, having helped himself
to oil (thinking it to be white vinegar) with his
oysters, he consumed them without a syllable of
complaint, and even with apparent relish.

This gentleman was so good as to show me his

left shoulder scarred in a hundred places by the claws of the leopards as they 'took off' it every day in their leaps, during the 'unparalleled performance of the wild leopard hunt.' He had the mark of a bite on his arm which cost a lion its life, and his proprietor three hundred pounds. 'It was a case of which was to go,' he said—'the lion or me—and I struck him over the nose with my loaded whip handle.' There is only one principle by which the wild beast world can be ruled, he told me—that of fear ; and should one of them once cease to fear him, he added, his life would not have been worth an hour's purchase. He had been twice dragged off insensible from an abortive performance of 'the Tiger King,' and only preserved from being torn to pieces by the interposition of a red-hot bar ; yet directly he recovered himself in he went again, whip in hand, and subdued the beasts. 'It was simply a question of showing myself their master then and there, or of giving up my situation.' He gave me these details (which were afterwards corroborated by the evidence of others) with great simplicity, and without the least approach to boastfulness ; and they interested me immensely. When this is the case with any subject, I have always found—after due consideration of the matter—that

O

I can make it interesting to my readers, and in the
' Family Scapegrace ' I scored my first success.   It
came out originally in serial form—as every novel
I have ever written has also done—and has passed
through many editions, but I believe it is as popular
to-day as it was twenty years ago.   For me, however, it has always a melancholy association, for the
brave young fellow who suggested it to me met, in
the end, with the fate which he had so long tempted.
He was not indeed, like the bad boy in the fable,
absolutely ' eaten by lions,' but he was killed by a
stroke of the paw of one, though the blow, I believe,
was not given in malice.   I am not sure whether
the publication of the ' Family Scapegrace ' in the
columns of the ' Journal ' increased its circulation,
but it was certainly well received.   Mr. William
Chambers, however, objected to it upon the ground
of its ' lightness.'   He would have preferred the
subject of wild beasts to have been more ' intelli-
gently treated ; ' their various habitats to be described, and some sort of moral to be deduced from
them ; but Robert stuck loyally to his young friend
and his story.

I took infinite pleasure in my editorial occupation, and had every reason to be content with my
surroundings.   My family, however, were delicate,

the climate of Edinburgh proved too vigorous for their constitutions, and after a year or two I was compelled to announce my intention of going south. Robert Chambers was so good as to express himself much concerned at this resolve, and characteristically endeavoured to combat it, upon the firm ground of science. 'You talk of cold, my dear sir, but let me tell you that the thermal line is precisely the same in Edinburgh as it is in London.' I replied, with as great truth as modesty, that I knew nothing about the thermal line, but that so far as I was aware the east wind had never blown a four-wheeled cab over in London—a circumstance which happened to have just taken place opposite our house in Edinburgh. As he saw my resolution was quite fixed, he presently said with a kind smile, 'I am thinking of going to live in London myself; suppose we go together, and you shall edit the " Journal" there instead of here.' Which struck me as a most excellent arrangement. The only drawback to my satisfaction was an undertaking I now entered into to confine my contributions to the 'Journal' only. It was not, indeed, an unreasonable requirement on his part, while it was in some sort a compliment to myself; but I regretted that my literary connection with 'Household Words,' or

rather with its chief, which had been so long and
constant, was now to cease ; that I was no longer to
serve under the banner of him whom Bret Harte,
in the most imperishable of his stories, has called
'The Master.'   I wrote, of course, to tell him of the
arrangement.   'I have received your letter,' he replied, 'with mingled regret and pleasure.   I am
heartily sorry to have lost you as a fellow-workman,
but heartily glad to have gained you as a friend.
. . . I hope that you will both [my wife and myself]
come and see us at Gadshill, and compare the
Kentish hops and cherries with the Scottish
peachings.'

CHAPTER VII.

LONDON—THE VALUE OF A TITLE—PERSONAL NARRA-
TIVES—AN EXECUTION—LEECH—GILBERT À BECKETT
—JAMES WHITE—READE—TROLLOPE—THACKERAY—
DICKENS.

IT was ill-naturedly said by Dr. Johnson that the
finest prospect that could meet the eyes of a Scotchman was the road to England ; and, though I was
no Scotchman, I felt something of this exhilaration
of spirit as I took my ticket from Edinburgh to
London.   It was not a single ticket by any means,
for we had a family sufficiently large to excuse our
having a saloon carriage to ourselves ; but their
numbers did not alarm me, for I had by that time
not only gained a footing in literature but was
confident of my power to climb.   Though I had
been born and bred far out of hearing of Bow Bells
and had only visited the metropolis occasionally, I
was extremely fond of it, mainly because it presents the broadest field of human life.   Young as

I was, I was already possessed with the conviction that for the calling I had chosen for myself London was the only place to live in, or at all events the best place ; and after a quarter of a century's experience I see no reason to change that opinion. The poet, the philosopher, and the man of science can live where they like, and pursue their studies equally well, but the novelist should reside where humanity presents its most varied aspect.

For years I studied London and the Londoners as a botanist studies the flora of his neighbourhood, and with unspeakable interest and delight ; I have written several works upon that subject only. One of them, ' Meliboeus in London,' is still a favourite, such as an author, unlike a father, is privileged to make of one of his own children without rousing the jealousy of the rest. Its publisher took the same view of it, and, much to his credit, always spoke of it in high terms, though it was, as regards the public favour, not so fortunate as the like offspring of the same pen. He ascribed its want of popularity to a cause which at that time I thought fanciful, but which I have long been persuaded was the right cause—namely, its title. ' It is not everybody,' he said, ' who has ever heard of Meliboeus, and those who have not are disinclined to inquire for him, because they don't know how to pronounce his name.'

Even Shakespeare occasionally erred, and never more so than when he wrote that celebrated dictum about the unimportance of a name. In books it has almost the same weight in this country as a title has in the case of an individual. A good name may not be 'better than riches' on the back of a good book, but it greatly enhances its pecuniary value. The name of the author, if he is a popular one, is also a tower of strength. Again and again have well-known writers, having composed a work which has especially taken their fancy, attempted to make a new departure with it, and by publishing it anonymously to gain a second reputation. Bulwer, for example, tried it, and Trollope tried it, both with unsatisfactory results. No one can afford to give up the momentum of their popularity and start afresh without it, up the hill. I hope I shall not be accused of comparing myself with the eminent writers I have mentioned in stating my own experience in this way.

Some years after I had obtained popularity I wrote a novel which I flattered myself was of considerable merit, and which I knew to be at least of greater merit than any which had preceded it from the same hand. It was called 'A Perfect Treasure.' In order to completely conceal my identity, I published it at the same time, and from the same house, as another novel under my own name called 'A County Family.' There was no comparison as to which was the better of the two books, and I will do the critics the justice to say that they perceived this. The former story was spoken of in high terms, and (just as I had hoped) as the production of a new author from whom great things were to be expected. The latter story was received less favourably—indeed (for there is a medium in all things), rather too consonantly with my expectations in that way. But when it came to balancing accounts matters were very different. 'If it had not been for the success of the "County Family,"' said the publisher, 'your "Perfect Treasure" would have let us into a hole.'

The omission of the author's name was of course the main factor in this unlooked-for result ; but even if both works had been anonymous, I am convinced, from the attraction of its title, that the 'County Family' would have shown a better balance than its more meritorious rival. Even in the case of so marvellously popular a writer as Dickens I have always thought that the want of

favour with which (at starting) ' Martin Chuzzlewit'
was received was to be attributed to its infelicitous
name. We are so accustomed nowadays to regard
it as one of his best, if not the very best of his
novels, and the name has been so long familiar to
us, that it is difficult to replace ourselves in the
position of having heard it for the first time ; but
such is to my mind the explanation of what is
otherwise little less than a literary phenomenon.

While on the subject of book titles I may say
that it is essential to choose one that has not been
used before. The law is in this matter very unreasonable, for, while establishing a copyright in
titles, it affords no means of discovering whether
the one you have decided upon is original or not.
While compelling an author to register his book in
Stationers' Hall, it makes no proviso for the
exhibition of the *name* of the book ; and, as the
register—from some miserable economy—only
shows the author's name, the information desired
cannot be obtained. Hence proceeds a regular
system of robbery. In the case of a known novel
of course there is no difficulty ; no author would
take ' Never Too Late to Mend ' or ' The Woman
in White ' for his title ; but a totally unknown book
may have a good name, which occurs quite natu-

rally to more than one person. Who can remember
the names of the still-born novels of the last forty
years? Nay, every week, there appears in the
'Penny Storyteller,' or the 'Penny Novelist,' some
tale the name of which is protected by copyright.
And what possible precaution can prevent this
right being involuntarily infringed?

Enterprising publishers of worthless books are
always on the look-out for a coincidence of this
kind, and exact their black-mail from the unfortunate author. There is no pretence of any
harm being done to them; indeed, nothing but
good, of course, can result to the still-born novel
from its having the same name as a new and
much better one; but the law is on the side of the
rogues. As I have written many novels, and have
been obliged to give them names, I have suffered
from this sharp practice more than most people.
I have given twenty pounds, and on one occasion
even forty pounds, for the privilege of calling my
own book by its own name; but that was when I
was comparatively a young writer. I should not
fall so easy a victim to these literary brigands now.
Though the law is, as I have said, unreasonable,
the judges are not so, and if any such case as I
have mentioned should be tried upon its merits I

should have no fear for the result. A trial is the very last thing that our persecutors desire ; what they want is ransom. My advice to my literary brethren is to resist all such extortioners ; it is not necessary to be rude to them ('the Court,' if the case proceeds, does not approve of that) ; instead of saying outright, ' Go to the devil,' use a synonym : refer them to a solicitor.

In a few years I knew my London better than most Cockneys born. On one occasion I compared my own experiences of it with those of Dickens. He told me in his graphic and dramatic way some amazing things, with some of which I, in my time, though with far inferior powers of narration, have occasionally thrilled a select audience. In return for his gold I had only silver to offer him, but I remember that the following incident, which once happened to me, interested him very much.

I was returning home one summer night through a fashionable street out of Piccadilly, when there came on a violent thunderstorm. It was very late, not a cab was to be seen, and I stepped under a portico for shelter. There was a ball going on in one of the great houses in the street ; the drawing-room had a huge bow-window, which was open, and now and again figures flitted across it, and the dance-music made itself heard through the storm. I had been under my shelter some time before I noticed that there was another person in the street, also under a portico. He was nearer to the house where the ball was going on than I was, but I could see him quite distinctly. He looked like a beggar and was dressed in rags. Suddenly he ran across the street in the pouring rain and stood beneath the open window, at which appeared some lady in a ball dress; she threw out to him her bouquet, the gilt handle of which I saw glitter in the gaslight. He strove to catch it, but it fell, and I heard it clang upon the pavement. He picked it up, nodded twice to the lady at the window, and then ran off at full speed. The whole thing took only a few seconds, but made a picture that I shall never forget.

I took it for granted that the man was her lover, and expressed to Dickens my astonishment at the perfection of the man's disguise.

'No,' he said, as though the facts were all before him, 'he was not her lover; he was merely a messenger waiting for the bouquet to be thrown to him, a signal that had been agreed upon beforehand.'

This conclusion I believe to have been the

correct one ; but I had forgotten, as usual, the precise date of the occurrence, and was therefore unable to discover from the newspapers whether any 'incident in high life' took place about the same time.

There was another experience of mine, which I should have narrated earlier, but which I now remember in connection with Dickens, for it especially tickled him. Speaking of the deep and narrow grooves in which life runs, and of the impossibility of its wheels ever getting out of them into other grooves, I told him the following anecdote. When I was quite a boy I happened to sit at a luncheon table between a lady of literary instincts and a sporting captain who was anxious to ingratiate himself with her; only, unhappily, they had not a single interest in common. At last he thought he had found one.

' Sad thing, Miss B——,' he suddenly remarked, ' about poor Sam Rogers.'

A robbery had just occurred at Rogers's bank, resulting in the loss of a very large sum of money.

'Yes, indeed,' returned the young lady sympathisingly ; 'however, it won't ruin him.'

' Well, I don't know—not so sure of that,' said the captain, pulling doubtfully at his moustache.

'It's a great blow, no doubt; but Rogers is very rich.'

'I think you are mistaken there,' he put in, 'though I dare say he has feathered his nest pretty well. It is a serious thing his being forbidden to ride for two years.'

'Forbidden to ride!' ejaculated the young lady, laying down her knife and fork in sheer astonishment. 'Why shouldn't he ride?'

'Well, because of what he has done, you know. The Jockey Club has suspended him.'

'The Jockey Club? Whom on earth, Captain L——, can you be talking about?'

'Why, about Sam Rogers, of course. Did I not *say* Sam Rogers—Sam Rogers the Jockey?'

A more complete example of cross purposes probably never occurred.

It so struck Dickens's fancy that I should not have been surprised had he made some literary use of it; but he had a very delicate sense of copyright, and probably thought that I might use it myself. It has always been a satisfaction to me, however, to believe that certain incidents I communicated to him, which had come within my private experience —and were therefore *taboo* so far as my own pen was concerned—were made excellent use of in

'Great Expectations,' where Miss Haversham appears for the second time to my eyes, as large as life indeed, but not one whit exaggerated.

In pursuit of my profession in town (for certainly I had no natural liking for such sights) I went to see the execution of the five pirates of the 'Flowery Land.' There was nothing in their case to excite pity. They had, without provocation, cast their captain and officers into the sea, and thrown champagne bottles at them while they were drowning. They were not, I am glad to say, Englishmen (they were natives of Manilla), but even if they had been I should have been in no way distressed at their fate.

Considering the universal unhappiness caused by the Cruel, one would be amazed that they are so lightly dealt with but for the reflection that our laws are made by those who do not suffer from their outrages. The life-long miseries they inflict upon those about them—defenceless women and children—are often far worse than murder ; and when they culminate in that crime it is almost a matter for congratulation, for the victim then is freed and the villain at last is hung. I have no sympathy whatever with the spurious philanthropy that would keep such wretches alive to be a curse to their fellow-creatures, but I am rejoiced that the just punishment of their brutality is no longer a public spectacle. The worst part of the execution to which I refer was not the hanging of the criminals, but the behaviour of the mob, to whom it was certainly no 'moral lesson.' Like Lord Tomnoddy I took a room with some friends (for which we paid twenty guineas) to see the sight. My description of it was thought too realistic for the ' Journal,' and, as at that date I had undertaken to write for no other periodical, it did not appear elsewhere. It is true it was afterwards published, but in an expensive form, and had few readers ; and, as public executions have long been things of the past, I give a short extract from it.

' At three o'clock or thereabouts there was heard a rumbling of some heavy carriage, and there broke forth a horrid yell, half cheer, half groan, from the people without. This was the arrival of the scaffold, a mere block of wood (to all appearance) painted black and drawn by three cart-horses. Then there ensued a horrid knocking, compared with which the knocking in "Macbeth" was but as the summons of a fashionable footman ; they were putting up the gallows. By this time the snow had begun to fall, flake by flake, but without diminishing the concourse ;

on the contrary, it grew and grew, so that the dawn
presently broke upon a pavement of human heads
extending as far as the eye could reach. Hats,
because they obstructed the view, were not permitted, and the effect of this sumptuary law was
certainly picturesque. Those who had been deprived of their head-gear had substituted for it
particoloured handkerchiefs, while caps of every
hue made the shifting scene like a pattern in a
kaleidoscope. Bakers' white caps, soldiers' blue caps,
provident persons' night-caps, and chimney sweepers'
black caps were now become very numerous, and
the mass of mere thieves and ruffians only leavened
the multitude instead of forming its sole constituents.
The chimney sweepers were extremely popular,
and encouraged to beat one another, so that the soot
should fly freely upon their neighbours ; and the
military were so far respected that I never saw one
of them pushed up from the surging crowd and
rolled lengthways over the heads of the company,
to which the members of all other professions were
continually subjected. Many gentlemen of volatile
dispositions (and of physical strength enough to
ensure impunity) would themselves leap upon the
shoulders of those about them and run along upon
all-fours on the surface of the crowd ; and nobody

P

seemed to resent it, even including the softer sex, except now and then a personal friend, who seemed to consider it as a liberty, although perfectly allowable in the case of strangers.

'I am sorry to say there were many women, although in no greater proportion to the males than one to ten. They were mostly young girls, who took no part in the rough amusements of their neighbours, unless under compulsion, but kept their gaze fixed on the Debtors' Door. One in particular, with roses in her bonnet and cruel eyes, never looked anywhere else : she reminded me horribly of the girl in Bulwer's " Last Days of Pompeii " who was so greedy to see the man devoured by the wild beast. No touch of pity, or even of awe, could be read in any countenance. When a black cloth, some two feet high, was placed round the edge of the scaffold, there was a yell of impotent rage, because a portion of the sight—the lowering of the dead bodies into their coffins—would be thereby lost to them. They cheered the hangman when he came out to adjust the ropes, as the herald of their coming treat ; they grew impatient as the clock grew near the stroke of eight, and some called, " Time !" I am afraid an idea crossed my mind that if all the people there present (except those at the windows) could be put out of the way, like those whose last agonies they had come to see, it would be no great loss.

'It is not eight o'clock, but it is very near. A little dog in danger of being trodden to death is rescued by the police, amid approbation, and placed in safety upon the pitching-block—where the porters rest their burdens—at the top of the street. That is a good sign; perhaps it is better to pity dogs than murderers. St. Sepulchre's bell begins to toll, although the inarticulate roar of voices almost drowns its solemn boom; there is a sharp and sudden cry of "Hats off!" and the particoloured carpet shows like a white sheet instantly. Where the barriers are not, in Newgate Street, the concourse bends and swells like the waves of a stormy sea; and where the barriers are, they are only distinguishable by their living burdens. There is a dreadful thronging of officials at the prison door, and five men are brought forth, one after another, to be strangled.

'Let us turn our backs upon that scene, my friends, if you please, and look rather upon the forty thousand eager faces receiving their moral lesson. They are not so impressed as to be silent—no, not for one instant—but emit a certain purring

satisfaction, like that of a cat over its prey. Then
a hiss breaks forth, and here and there the word
" cur " is heard—that is because one of the wretched
victims has fainted, and must needs be seated in a
chair—and then there is a tempest of applause
because the fifth man goes to his doom with as
jaunty an air as his pinioned arms will permit. The
priest is speaking the last few words that these
wretches shall hear from mortal tongue ; they are
kissing (through those terrible caps) the crucifix he
holds in his hand, and in a few seconds they will
have crossed the threshold of life and entered upon
the mysteries of eternity. Surely if the moral lesson
is to give any visible sign of its working it must be
now. It gives no sign whatever. The babblement
never ceases ; there is no hush, no reverence, no fear.
Only after a certain dreadful grinding noise—which
is the fall of the drop—a flood of uproar suddenly
bursts forth, which must have been pent up before.
This, the truth is, is the collective voice of the
Curious, the Fast, the Vicious, spell-bound for a
little by the awful spectacle, while the ceaseless
though lesser din arises from the professional
scoundrels, the thieves *in esse*, the murderers *in
posse*, who are impressed by nothing save by the
touch of the fatal slip-knot under their own right

ears. Singularly enough, the crowd increased after
the execution, persons of delicate temperament
joining it, I suppose, who had not nerve enough
for a hanging, but who knew how to appreciate a
cutting down.'

It has often been said that Dickens was in
favour of the abolition of capital punishment. It
was certainly not the case at this date, nor do I
believe it ever was, though he wrote strongly
against public executions. Speaking of the vil-
lainous crew of the ' Flowery Land,' he told me
that the sheriff had given him a very characteristic
account of them. There had been originally seven
condemned to death, but two were reprieved.
Reprieved criminals are generally much affected,
and the fact of their escape is broken to them with
great care by the officials. In this case, when the
two men were told they were not to be hung, one
received the news with total apathy, but the other
with great vivacity exclaimed, ' Then can I have
Antonio's shoes ' (Antonio was one of his less
fortunate friends), ' because they exactly fit me ? '

Dickens had been present at the execution of
Mrs. Manning and knew something of the lady.
With the exception of Mrs. Brownrigg she was
perhaps the wickedest of her sex ; but she had her

attractions. He told me that when arrested in Edinburgh she so worked upon the feelings of the police officer that accompanied her in the train to town—though he was an elderly man with a family —that he could never forgive himself the hand he had in her subsequent fate, and that when she was executed he committed suicide. The effigy of her in Madame Tussaud's, in Baker Street, was very like, and I went to see it in consequence. The great annual cattle show was being held under the same roof, and I remember—such was my eye to 'copy' at that time—that I wrote an account of both exhibitions on the occasion, under the not inappropriate title of 'Wax and Tallow.'

It was about this period that the 'Comic History of England' was being published, with its admirable illustrations by Leech. I often met that artist, a gentle pleasant fellow, beloved by all who knew him, but certainly one who disappointed expectation in the way of comedy. He was very silent, and his air was generally one of settled gloom. He was, no doubt, however, a great observer, and when he heard a lively story that 'lent itself' to illustration he would sometimes inquire 'whether it was copyright.'

Gilbert à Beckett I only met once, at a little

dinner party given by one of the founders of
' Punch ;' his talk was very entertaining and characteristic. There was some guava jelly at dessert,
which pleased my youthful palate. ' I am glad you
like it,' said my hostess. 'We rather plume ourselves upon it. Some people make it of apple and
call it guava; they think there is no harm in a false
name.'

' You should rather say an appellation,' murmured à Beckett.

The Reverend James White I have already
mentioned. I had known him in my boyhood, at
Shanklin, where we used to crack jokes together,
though mine of course were hazel nuts (and often
with nothing in them), while his were from the
cocoa-tree. He had a kindly as well as a humorous
nature, and protected me from the many snubs (I
dare say well deserved) which my precocity evoked
from my elders. Detraction, flickering with its
serpent tongue, went so far as to say that he spoilt
me ; a statement which bore falsehood on the face
of it. He was the first man I knew who was intimate with literary men and who told me anecdotes
about them. He was a great friend of Dickens
and of Tennyson. I remember his reciting to me
a sonnet the latter had written, describing a sail he

and White and Peel (the author of 'The Fair Island') took together one day. Respect for the laws of copyright, and also my forgetfulness of all the lines but one, prevent my quoting the entire poem ; but the first line, I remember, ran thus :

'Two poets and a mighty dramatist,'

at the utterance of which last word he struck his breast theatrically and observed parenthetically, 'That's *me*, young gentleman.' Indeed, White's dramas from Scottish history were of great merit, and one of them, ' The King of the Commons,' was played by Macready (at the Princess's) with great success.   He also wrote ' The Landmarks of English History,' ' Eighteen Christian Centuries,' and a very good ' History of France.'   I have heard that when at Oxford, though too lazy to write for ' the Newdigate,' he converted in a single evening the severely classical poem that gained the prize into something, if not superior, at all events, very different, by interpolating alternate lines of the most humorous character ; and the high spirits of his youth very frequently asserted themselves in maturity.   I remember his reproving a very talkative young woman for her garrulity at the same time that he corrected her grammar.   They were going in to dinner one day, and he expressed his hope that she had a good appetite.

'I always have,' she said ; ' my motto is *toujours prêt.*'

'It should be *toujours prête,* my dear,' was her companion's reply.

He was an excellent story-teller, and I well remember his describing to me a particular evening with Douglas Jerrold, and some social wits, which made me yearn to be in such company. It was at the time of some threatened French invasion, and one man (he told me) announced his intention of ' locking himself in the cellar and arming himself with a corkscrew ; ' another, who had taken a sufficiency of champagne, of 'joining the Toxophilite Society,' whereupon Jerrold flashed out, like a rapier from its sheath, that the *In*toxophilite Society would better suit him.

The novelist last taken from us, Charles Reade, I saw less of than of his literary brethren. My acquaintance with him did not begin till his infirmity of deafness had grown to be a source of much inconvenience to him ; but it certainly had not the effect, often attributed to it, of making him impatient or morose. His hollowed hand and smiling, attentive face are always present in the

picture which my memory draws of him.   He
expressed himself very strongly upon matters in
which his feelings were moved, but they were always
moved in the right direction, and though, when
contending with an adversary on paper, he did not
use the feather end of his pen, his heart was as soft
as a woman's.   He was never moved by those petty
jealousies which (with little reason, so far as my
experience goes) are attributed to his craft, and the
last time he spoke to me on literary subjects was
in praise of one who might well have been considered a rival—Wilkie Collins.   ' I can imagine,' he
said, ' that his work fails to appeal to some people,
otherwise good judges, but he is a great artist.'

The last time I saw him he was painfully
ascending the stairs of the London Library, looking very old and ill.   I waited for him on the
landing, where he noticed some books in my hand
which I was carrying away for a professional
purpose.

' How hard you work !' he said ; then added
with pathos, ' so did I at your age.'

His tone and manner recalled to me those of
another and greater writer on an occasion when I
was instancing to him Walter Scott's inability to
compose when he wished to do so, and his bursting

into tears in consequence, as the most pathetic incident in the annals of literature. 'For God's sake don't talk of it,' he said, ' it is what we must all come to.' But he never did come to it, nevertheless.

Lever I met very seldom, and never when he was at his best. He had fallen into ill health and premature old age. Yet at times he was a charming companion ; not a conversationalist, but an admirable *raconteur.* When once set a-going he fairly bubbled over with good stories ; but they were for the most part Irish and connected with old times. He had lived so long out of England that he was not *en rapport* with people and things of the day. His nature was as genial and careless as that of the heroes of his earlier books, and he had no notion of practical affairs even when connected with his own calling. He told me, only a few years before his death, that he had never received sixpence from the sale of his advanced sheets anywhere. To me, whom circumstances compelled to look after such matters pretty keenly, and who, if I had not 'surveyed mankind from China to Peru' with an eye to advanced sheets, had 'placed' them on occasion even in Japan (at Yokohama), this neglect appeared inexplicable.

It is probable that his publishers made these outside arrangements for him, and took them into account in their transactions with him. In Trollope's case, who told me almost the same thing —'I never got a farthing from the Americans,' he said, 'save 50*l.* for "Ayala's Angel"'—it seems certain that he laboured under the same mistake, a far more extraordinary one for *him* to make, who plumed himself upon his business habits, than for Lever. It may be of interest to the public (as it certainly will be to the budding novelist) to learn that the serial works of our popular writers appear coincidently not only in America, but in many of our colonies.[1] Australia is the most liberal and enterprising in this respect, and Canada (a fact which is partly explained by its being overshadowed by

---

[1] The following case, by no means an uncommon one, illustrates the system of 'distribution' as regards fiction which now prevails. A novel is published in serial by a 'syndicate' of eight or ten provincial newspapers, the Saturday issues of which (in which it appears) have an average circulation say of 25,000. The novel simultaneously appears in America and Australia, say in *Harper's Weekly* and the *Australasian*, which have both immense circulations. This gives at least 300,000 buyers; but it is calculated, with good reason, taking into account the family, the club, the mechanics' institute, and friends to whom the novel may be lent, that there are six readers for every buyer. Thus the readers of the popular novelist of to-day may literally be reckoned by millions. Moreover, this does not include the readers of the various editions of the book itself, or of its translations.

the Great Republic) the least. The works of our story-tellers are also to be found in every European tongue : with **Russia,** Holland, **and** Sweden there is, however, no international copyright, so that no- thing is to be got out of them but thanks and fame ; and with **France** and Italy, although there is a treaty, there **might** almost as well not be one, so far as any material benefit to the English author is con- cerned. Germany, however, though poor, is honest, and sends some slight contribution to the British author's purse in return for the right of translation.

The edition of Baron Tauchnitz, which is of course in English, is quite another affair. There is a notion abroad—or rather at home—that the Baron does not purchase the works he publishes in his Continental series. **This is a gross mistake.** He did so even when there was no necessity (i.e. when there was no copyright treaty, as he does now in the case of American authors), and I have always **found him** to be not only an honourable but a most liberal paymaster.

Trollope was the least literary man of letters I ever **met ;** indeed, had I not known him for the large-hearted and natural man he was, I should have suspected him of some affectation in this respect. **Though** he certainly took pleasure in

writing novels I doubt whether he took any in
reading them ; and from his conversation, quite as
much as from his own remarks on the subject in
his autobiography, I should judge he had not read
a dozen, even of Dickens's, in his life. His manners
were rough and, so to speak, tumultuous, but he
had a tender heart and a strong sense of duty. He
has done his literary reputation as much harm by
the revelation of his method of work as by his
material views of its result. He took almost a
savage pleasure in demolishing the theory of
'inspiration,' which has caused the world to deny
his 'genius ; ' but although he was the last, and a
long way the last, of the great triumvirate of
modern novelists (for Bulwer is not to be named in
the same breath and George Eliot stands *per se*), he
hangs ' on the line ' with them.

If I may venture to express my own opinion
upon a matter to which I have at least given more
attention than most people, there seems to me
this noteworthy difference between the above-
named three authors and their living contemporaries : the characters they have drawn are more
individualised. Dick Swiveller, Colonel Newcome,
and Mrs. Proudie, for example, are people we know
and speak of as having had a real existence,

The works of other novelists are (with certain exceptions, however, for who does not recall Count Fosco ?) known by their names rather than by the characters they have created.

I take, merely as a specimen (and I trust Mr. Blackmore will forgive me for so doing), that admirable romance 'Lorna Doone ;' none of the three men we are considering could have written it to save their lives, yet I doubt whether ten of the thousands of readers who have delighted in it could give the names of its *dramatis personæ*. There is nothing so cheap (and nasty) as detraction ; and in stating this opinion, detraction is the last thing, Heaven knows, which I wish to convey. I have the heartiest contempt for that school of critic-asters (as Charles Reade called them) who are always praising the dead at the expense of the living ; and there are probably few readers who take such pleasure in the works of living writers as I do. There is, I readily admit, more poetry and natural truth in some of them than in Dickens ; more dramatic interest than in Thackeray ; more humour and pathos than in Trollope ; but, to my mind, the individualism of character is much less marked than in those three authors.

I first saw Thackeray at the house of my

brother-in-law,[1] with whom I was then staying in Gloucester Place; they had lived together as young men at Weimar, but had never seen one another since, and their meeting was very interesting. Their lines in life had been very different, but the recollection of old times drew them together closely. A curious and characteristic thing happened on the occasion in question. There were a dozen people or so at dinner, all unknown to Thackeray, but he was in good spirits and made himself very agreeable. It disappointed . me excessively, when, immediately after dinner, he informed me that he had a most particular engagement and was about to wish good night to his host. 'But will you not even smoke a cigar first?' I inquired. 'A cigar? Oh, they smoke here, do they? Well, to tell you the truth, that *was* my engagement,' and he remained for many hours. There was an ancient gentleman at table who had greatly distinguished himself half a century ago at college, by whom the novelist was much attracted, and especially when he told him that there was nothing really original in modern literature; everything, he

---

[1] Major Prower. At his home, Purton House, in Wiltshire, I spent many of the happiest days of my early life; would that his eye could note the acknowledgment!

said, came indirectly more or less from—I think he
said—Pindar.

'But at all events Pindar did not write "Vanity
Fair,"' I said.

'Yes, sir,' answered the old gentleman, 'he
did. In the highest and noblest sense Pindar did
write it.'

This view of affairs, which was quite new to
him, delighted Thackeray, who was so pleased
with his evening that he invited the whole company
—fourteen in all—to dine with him the next day.
I mention the circumstance not only as being a
humorous thing in itself, but as illustrative of a
certain boyish and impulsive strain that there was
in his nature. He told me afterwards that when
he subsequently went to the club that night he had
felt so dangerously hospitable that it was all he
could do to prevent himself 'asking some more
people;' and as a matter of fact he did ask two
other guests. He had been very moderate as to
wine-drinking, and was only carried away by a
spirit of geniality, which now and then overmastered
him. The guests who had so much taken his fancy
—or perhaps it was only the ancient Classic, whom
he could not well have invited without the others
—were of course delighted with their invitation,

but many of them had scruples about accepting it.
They called the next afternoon, in pairs, to know
'what we were going to do about it,' and 'whether
we thought Mr. Thackeray had really meant it.'
For my part, I said I should go if I went alone ;
and go we did.   An excellent dinner we got, notwithstanding the shortness of the notice ; nor in
our kind hostess's manner could be detected the
least surprise at what must nevertheless have
seemed a somewhat unlooked-for incursion.

Trollope has been hard on Thackeray—just as
the public have been hard on Trollope—because
his mode of composition did not chime in with
his own, and was indeed diametrically opposite.
Thackeray's habits were anything but methodical,
and he found the duties of editorship especially
irksome.   Communications from his contributors,
and especially the would-be ones, annoyed and even
distressed him to an almost incredible degree.   I
remember his complaining of one of them with a
vigour and irritation which amused me exceedingly.
A young fellow had sent him a long story, for
which he demanded particular attention 'from the
greatest of novelists,' upon the ground that he had
a sick sister entirely dependent upon him for
support.   Thackeray was touched by the appeal,

and, contrary to his custom, wrote his correspondent a long letter of advice, enclosing also (which was by no means contrary to his custom) some pecuniary assistance. 'I feel for your position,' he said, 'and appreciate your motive for exertion ; but I must tell you at once that you will never do anything in literature. Your contribution is worthless in every way, and it is the truest kindness, both to her for whom you are working and to yourself, to tell you so outright. Turn your mind at once to some other industry.'

This produced a reply from the young gentleman which astonished Thackeray a great deal more than it did me. It was couched in the most offensive terms conceivable, and ended by telling 'the greatest of novelists' that, though he had attained by good luck 'the top of the tree, he would one day find himself, where he deserved to be, at the bottom of it.'

'For my part,' said Thackeray (upon my showing some premonitory symptoms of suffocation), 'I see little to laugh at. What a stupid, ungrateful beast the man must be ! and if ever I waste another half hour again in writing to a creature of that sort " call me horse," or worse.' He was not so ac-

customed to the vagaries of rejected contributors
as I was.

Though the views of life entertained by Dickens
and Thackeray were as different as the poles, it
has always been the fashion to draw comparisons
between them ; some disciples of the latter have
even thought they did their master honour by
speaking of Dickens as his rival and then depre-
ciating him.   I wonder whether these gentry knew
what Thackeray really thought of Dickens's genius.
They certainly could hardly have read what he
wrote of it, and especially of the pathetic side
of it.

'And now,' says Thackeray (I think in his ' Box
of Christmas Books '), ' there is but one book left
in the box, the smallest one ; but oh, how much
the best of all !   It is the work of the master of
all English humorists now alive—the young man
who came and took his place calmly at the head of
the whole tribe, and who has kept it.   Think of all
we owe him—the store of happy hours that he has
made us pass ; the kindly and pleasant companions
whom he has introduced to us ; the harmless
laughter, the genial wit, the frank, manly love he
has taught us to feel.   Every month of these years
has brought us some kind token from this delight-

ful genius. . . . What books have appeared that have taken so affectionate a hold of our English public as his ? '

Of the 'Carol' he wrote : ' Who can listen to objections regarding such a book as this ? It seems to me a national benefit, and to every man and woman who reads it a personal kindness. The last two people I heard speak of it were women ; neither knew the other, or the author, and both said by way of criticism, " God bless him ! " . . . As for Tiny Tim, there is a certain passage in the book regarding that young gentleman about which a man should hardly speak in print, or in public, any more than he would of any other affliction of his private heart. There is not a reader in England but that little creature will be a bond of union between author and him ; and he will say of Charles Dickens, as the women did just now, " God bless him ! " What a feeling is this for a writer to be able to inspire, and what a reward to reap ! '

Lest it should be imagined that this opinion of Thackeray's respecting the merits of his great con- temporary was extorted by his admiration of his 'Christmas Books' alone, or was expressed upon his earlier writings only, I append a much later and less known criticism to the same effect.

'As for the charities of Mr. Dickens, multiplied
kindnesses which he has conferred upon us all, upon
our children, upon people educated and uneducated,
upon the myriads who speak our common tongue,
have not you, have not I, all of us, reason to be
thankful to this kind friend who so often cheered
so many hours, brought pleasure and sweet laughter
to so many homes, made such multitudes of children
happy, endowed us with such a sweet store of
gracious thoughts, fair fancies, soft sympathies,
hearty enjoyments? I may quarrel with Mr.
Dickens's art a thousand and a thousand times ; I
delight and wonder at his genius. I recognise it—
I speak with awe and reverence—a commission from
that Divine Beneficence whose blessed task we
know it will one day be to wipe every tear from every
eye. Thankfully I take my share of the feast of
love and kindness which this noble and generous
and charitable soul has contributed to the happiness of the world. I take and enjoy my share,
and say a benediction for the meal.'

I should especially recommend this criticism to
'the drawing-rooms and the clubs'—the people who
don't think and the people who don't feel—when
they are inclined to speak of Dickens's 'morbid
sentimentality.'

While I am upon this subject, I cannot refrain from saying a word or two about the insolence, not of the critics—for I have already expressed my high opinion both of their ability and **their appreciativeness**—but of a certain class of amateur critics in relation to fiction. 'Everyone can poke a fire and drive a gig,' and, it would also seem, can criticise a novel. 'Although,' says Miss Austen, speaking of her own trade, 'our productions have afforded more extensive and unaffected pleasure than those of any other literary corporation in the world, no species of composition has been so much decried. From pride, ignorance, and fashion our foes are almost as many as our readers, and while the abilities of the nine hundred and ninety-ninth abridger of the History of England are eulogised by a thousand pens, there seems a general agreement to slight the performances which have only genius, wit, and taste to recommend them.'

Novelists are certainly not 'slighted' now, but 'the nine hundred and ninety-ninth abridger,' or anyone else who has distinguished himself in quite another line of literature, thinks himself qualified to sit in judgment upon the genius of Dickens. Only a few months ago I read a criticism (as I suppose he would call it) from a person of this kind, to whom no one ever imputed the possession of a single grain of humour or pathos, which may well serve as a warning to all such trespassers upon a domain of which they know absolutely nothing. 'I could never read Dickens with any pleasure,' he candidly confesses, without the least consciousness of writing himself down an ass; and then he proceeds to discuss his works. Of course there are many intelligent persons to whom the power of appreciating fiction of any kind is denied; what is amazing is that they should rush into print to say so. Their opinion should be entertained in silence, or expressed to their friends as it were *in camerâ*, so that the fact of their intellectual incompetency should be concealed. What Thackeray—a well-qualified critic indeed—wrote of Dickens he also certainly felt. I had once a long conversation with him upon the subject: it was before the shadow (cast by a trivial matter after all) had come between them, but I am sure that would not have altered his opinion. Of course there were some points on which he was less enthusiastic than on others; the height of the literary pedestal on which Dickens stood was, he thought, for some reasons, to be deplored for his own sake. 'There is nobody to tell him when anything goes wrong,' he said; 'Dickens is the Sultan, and Wills is his Grand Vizier ¡' but, on the whole, his praise was as great as it was generous.

It is a satisfaction to me to remember that our two great novelists became friends again before death took all that it could take of one of them away ; I walked back with the survivor from the other's funeral at Kensal Green, and from what Dickens said on that occasion—though the touching 'In Memoriam' from his pen in the 'Cornhill' was proof sufficient—I can bear witness to the fact.

CHAPTER VIII.

PUBLISHERS AND AUTHORS—ANONYMOUS PUBLICATIONS
—LITERARY GAINS—TWO IMPOSTORS—WHIST—FAME.

I WAS thirty-two years of age, and had written
many books and a very large number of miscel-
laneous articles, before I made my first success in
literature. I had advanced, I think, as regards the
art of story-telling, and certainly in public favour,
but only in a moderate way. There had been no
'leaps and bounds' in my progress ; but the appearance of ' Lost Sir Massingberd ' was an epoch in my
literary life. The idea (as I have mentioned elsewhere) occurred to me on the top of a coach ; and it
was the best day's journey I ever took. The story
appeared, of course, in the 'Journal,' and very
largely increased its circulation. Its proprietors—
for in such a case it would be ungenerous to dis-
sociate them—behaved with great liberality towards
me. I mention the matter (though some may
consider it a private one) not only because it reflects
credit on the firm in question, but because it casts
some light on the relation between publishers and

authors generally. There is a notion abroad that
the latter are almost invariably the victims of the
former, and that, while Justice has but a legal
foothold in Paternoster Row, Generosity has none
at all. My experience, which on such matters is
probably as large as that of any man alive, is to
the contrary of all this. There are bad publishers
of course, skinflints ('scaly varmints,' as a cab-
driver once called a friend of mine, who was so
delighted with the term that he at once gave him
half-a-sovereign), but in what other profession are
such characters unknown? I have met with some
sharp practice with publishers myself, and have
never hesitated to say so, or to give piquancy to
the narrative by the disclosure of their names;
but such experiences have been quite exceptional.
Upon the whole I am convinced that I have been
handsomely treated.

Talking of this subject upon one occasion with
a brother novelist, he gave me the following extract
from his literary note-book. 'My first work,' he
said, 'was published by Blank & Co., who gave me
a decent sum for the first edition, not one half of
which was sold. When I became popular I disposed of the copyright of the volume elsewhere,
and feeling indebted to them for their liberality,

and also sorry for their loss, I sent them half the money I received for the book. You never saw such a letter as Blank sent me. One would have thought I had given him a fortune instead of only a small portion of what I had lost him. He could not have expressed more astonishment if it had dropped from the clouds.'

I have no doubt Mr. Blank was very much astonished. And yet it is far from uncommon for publishers to give very considerable sums to successful authors beyond what they have bargained for. Of course it may be urged—for there are some people who never will give the devil his due —that this has been done as a retaining fee in order to keep their clients. I can only say that I have known cases where such a motive could not possibly have been imputed, and as they have happened—among others—to myself, I may venture to be quite positive upon the point.

While upon the subject of publishers, I will narrate a story told me by one of that useful and innocuous class called Readers. He was in the great house of Paternoster, Row and Co., but (one cannot but think fortunately for him) Row was dead. One day my friend received one of those charming *brochures* so common now-a-days, full of ill-natured gossip about literature and its disciples. Among other disagreeable things, it said that that eminently successful work ' Disloyala : or the Doubtful Priest,' which had run through fifty editions, had been rejected by his house some years ago. He showed this libel with much indignation to his friend and employer, Mr. Paternoster.

' Is not this,' he cried, ' an infamous statement ? '

' What *does* it matter ? ' was the quiet reply ; ' this sort of gentleman will say anything.'

' But I really can't stand it,' persisted the Reader. 'It is a gross libel upon us both, but especially upon me ; I shall write to the man and give him a piece of my mind.'

' I wouldn't do that if I were you,' said Mr. Paternoster, still more quietly than before.

' But why not ? I really must——'

There was a twinkle in Mr. Paternoster's eye, and a smile at the extreme corners of his mouth, which attracted the other's attention, and interrupted his eloquence.

' Is there any reason why I should not contradict this man ? '

' Well, yes ; the fact is, we did reject the book.'

' What ? Do you mean to say I rejected ' Disloyala " ? '

'I am afraid so ; at all events, we did it amongst us. I don't blame you ; I think it even now a dullish book.'

'And you never told me ?   Never let fall a word of it all these years ? '

'Certainly not. I thought it might distress you. I should not have told you now, but that I was taken unawares.'

This to my mind is one of the prettiest stories I have ever heard. I should like to see the General who could be equally reticent, when the Chief of his Intelligence Department had omitted a precaution that would have secured him a victory ; or the Solicitor who had lost his cause through the neglect of his Counsel ; or the Politician who had missed his point in the House through the short-coming of his Secretary.   Yet Mr. Paternoster was a publisher, one of that fraternity who, if we are to believe some people, are incapable of a generosity. For my part (who have collected a considerable number of anecdotes of the human race) I have never heard a more creditable story, even of a Divine.

Dissatisfaction with honest publishers indeed rarely takes place, except with very young authors. These have great confidence in their own work, and when it does not succeed are prone to blame everybody but themselves. But the fact is, even if a new book is a good book, it is very rarely successful. To make it known to the public requires advertising, and that process is expensive, and soon swallows up a small profit, even if profit is made. Upon the whole, it behoves the young author to look upon his first venture as itself an advertisement, and not reckon to make his fortune by it. And yet if it be successful, even if it does not 'pay' (for the things are quite compatible), it may really make his fortune ; for it paves the way (although not with gold) for its successor. My own experience of this matter has been already narrated. I had very good reason to be satisfied with my first production, though it was a pecuniary loss. On the other hand, I did not achieve by it any sudden reputation.

'Lost Sir Massingberd' was, I think, my fourth book ; from that time my position as a story-writer was secure, and I began to receive considerable sums for my books. Even then, however, my progress, though always upward, was slow, and it must have been at least ten years before I reached those 'four figures' which are supposed in the literary market to indicate the position of the 'popular author.' After that, things bettered

with me, and much more rapidly; but what a
beggarly account do the profits of literature present
beside those of successful men at the bar, in
medicine, or in trade! The most popular novelist
alive does not realise per annum what is every
year pocketed by a second-rate barrister, or a
physician in moderate practice. His term of
prosperity is also shorter, for the gift of imagination
generally fails us long before those talents which are
sufficient for ordinary intellectual toil. And yet
nothing is more common than to hear otherwise
sensible people talk of the large incomes made by
popular writers.

Trollope and Scott were exceptionally quick
workers, but there are few men who can write a
three-volume novel, worth reading, under nine
months; in the same time a popular painter can
produce at least three pictures, for each of which
he gets as large a sum as the popular writer for his
entire book. Nor does his work take out of the
artist as it does out of the author. Indeed, if a
man looks for wealth, the profession of literature
is the very last I would recommend him to embrace.
On the other hand, such guerdon as the novelist
does receive is gained very pleasantly and accompanied by many charming circumstances. He can

choose his society where he likes, for all doors are open to him. If fool enough to prefer swelldom to comfort, he has no need to struggle for it, as men in other callings with ten times his income must needs do. At the tables of the great he is not placed according to the degrees of rank (or Heaven knows where he would be), but enjoys a status of his own. In ordinary society, too (which is much more 'particular' than the 'best circles'), he is regarded with an exceptional charity. His position, indeed, among the most respectable people always reminds me of a lunatic among the Indians : 'the Great Spirit' has afflicted him with genius, they think (or at all events with something of that nature), and it behoves them to wink at his little infirmities. Nobody dreams of asking whether he is High Church, or Low Church, or even No Church. However much he may be 'at his ease in Zion,' nobody accuses him of irreverence. It has been said of a certain personage that a great many more people know T. F—— than T. F—— knows ; but the number of people who want to know your popular novelist is almost incredible. His photograph is sighed for by literary maidens beyond the seas, and by professional photographers (who take him for nothing) at home; his autograph is demanded

R

from some quarter of the world by every post.
Poems are written on him, books are dedicated to
him, paragraphs about his failing health (often when
he is quite well, which makes it the more pleasant)
pervade the newspapers, as though he were a bishop
who gives hopes of a vacant see. If vanity is his
ruling passion (a circumstance not altogether un-
precedented), he should indeed be a happy man.

What, however, he is really to be congratulated
upon is his work itself, which, always delightful to
him, can be pursued anywhere and at any time ;
he is tied to no place, and can take holiday when
and where he will ; while, above all, the nature of
his occupation brings him into connection with the
pleasantest and brightest people. In this last respect, if in no other—for my little book, though a
successful story, made no great noise in the world
—I had reason to be grateful to 'Lost Sir Massingberd.' It attracted the attention of some of my
masters in the art of fiction, and among them that
of my friend Wilkie Collins. He has probably
long forgotten the gracious words which he bestowed
upon it, but I remember them as though they were
spoken yesterday instead of twenty years ago.
Accustomed as was the author of 'The Moon-
stone' to strike at the root of a mystery, he told me

that he could not guess what had become of my missing baronet—in which lies what dramatic interest the book possesses—till he came on the page that told him. My old friend at The Knoll of course wrote to congratulate me, though my story, she said, was far too exciting for her, and in her failing health had given her more discomfort than pleasure ; and Dickens touched my trembling ears with praise. What was really remarkable about the book was that I had, of course uncon- sciously, taken for the name of my hero the very name (Massingberd) of a gentleman who had been missing for years, and to this day (I believe) has never been heard of by his friends.

Among those in another sphere of life with whom literature has brought me into connection was the late lamented Duke of Albany. Years ago, long before he took that title, one of my works was so fortunate as to beguile some hours of pain, and led to my introduction to him. I visited him at Boyton Manor, the house he had in Wiltshire, and subsequently at Claremont, and elsewhere. He was a most cordial and kindly host, and never could have been mistaken, even by the most cynical nature, for a patron. His love of literature was so great and genuine as to excuse my mention of him

in this place, even if the interest attaching to his
memory were less deep and general. He had an
hereditary talent for languages, and the passion of
his race for music. These things were lost upon
me, and he knew it, and (as if I had been the
Prince and he the Courtier) took pains to avoid
those topics in my company. It was the same in
politics, in which we had not an opinion in common.
I remember visiting him at the time of the Turco-
Russian war, and he observed on receiving me (in
playful reference to my wrong-headedness in other
matters), ' I do hope, Payn, you are at least a good
Turk.' And when I was obliged to shake my
head, he said, ' Well, then, we won't talk about it ; '
and we never did. If this courteous reticence were
more generally observed, a new charm would often
be given to hospitality. As a host, indeed, Prince
Leopold was almost faultless. He never forgot,
however great might be the interval between their
visits, the little peculiarities of his friends. In
royal residences the early hours, which are essential
to my private comfort, are not usual, nor is it
customary to retire before the master of the house.
But long before it grew late he would make some
pleasant observation about the habits of those who
were not night birds, which left me free to go to

roost. He was not a student in the ordinary sense of the word, though his knowledge of science and philosophy was probably much superior to mine, but he was well acquainted with the lighter branches of literature, and took great pleasure in them. I had the satisfaction of introducing him to the works of Lefanu, and his admiration of that author (so strangely neglected by the general public, notwithstanding the popularity of some of his imitators) vied with my own. He was fond of humour, though not of the boisterous kind (which perhaps requires physical health for its appreciation), and his favourite modern author was Thackeray. In Scott, too, he took great delight, and pointed out to me with pride a memento which had been given him by his hostess at Abbotsford, the bog oak walking-stick which Sir Walter brought away with him from Ireland, and of which he made such constant use. He had had his choice of richer relics, but had the good taste and sense to know what to choose.

'Lost Sir Massingberd' (which W. G. Clark *would* always call 'Found Sir Missing Bird') was published, like many of its successors, anonymously, an example which I would earnestly dissuade my literary brethren from following. If one has any

246 SOME LITERARY RECOLLECTIONS.

personalty belonging to one (whether it is spelt with
an *i* or not), it is just as well to claim it, otherwise
some one is sure to do so. A literary gentleman
in Glasgow, upon the strength of the authorship of
this very book of mine, collected money from the
charitable for some weeks. He said that the writer
of the work in question had been very ill re-
munerated, and appealed with confidence to the
spirit of fair play inherent in every British breast.
Nay, curiously enough, so late as last year there
was another Richmond in the field ; for my friend
Walter Besant writes to me from a North-country
inn as follows : 'I met a man in the coffee-room
here who gave me many mysterious hints of his
great position in the world of letters, and, finding
him very anxious to be interrogated, took care
not to trouble him with any questions. I asked
the landlady, however, who he was. " Oh ! " said
she, " he is quite a famous literary gent ; he wrote
'A Confidential Agent.' " ' My correspondent con-
cludes his letter : 'I have always suspected this ;
he is a much more distinguished-looking fellow,
and more likely to have done it than you.' Such
are the so-called friendships between literary men
in the same line of business.

Speaking of impostors reminds me of two very

fine specimens with whom, about this time, I became acquainted, one of whom adorned, and, for all I know to the contrary, may still adorn, my own profession. One evening a gentleman called at my house and requested to see me upon very particular business. As I was absent from home, he asked to see my wife. He was a gentlemanly-looking person of delicate appearance, and very shy, hesitating manners. ' It is most unfortunate,' he stammered, 'for they told me at the office I should be sure to find Mr. Payn at home, and he is the only friend in London on whom I can rely under certain circumstances—pressing ones—in which I find myself.'

' You know my husband, then ? '

'No, Madam, I do not ; but my name—Henslow —would not be unfamiliar to him. I am a novelist, and the author of a serial now running in the " Phœnix Magazine." '

His hostess smiled politely, but could not go so far as to say that we took in the ' Phœnix.' Could she give any message for him to her husband ?

He shook his head. ' The fact is, Madam, my difficulty is very urgent ; it is of a domestic and not of a literary character. I came up to town from Gloucestershire this morning with my poor

sister to consult a London physician upon her
account. She is dying, but there are hopes of
alleviation and mitigation. At Swindon Station I
got out to get her some refreshment, and left my
purse on the counter. We are absolutely without
a penny between us.'

'Good heavens! But where *is* your sister?'

'She is in the second-class ladies' waiting-room
at Paddington Station. She has been there for
eight hours. I have been all day waiting for the
only acquaintance I had in town, but in vain.
Then I thought of your husband, who, being of the
same calling, and knowing me at least by name,
would, I felt sure, lend me a few shillings.'

The question to have asked, no doubt, would
have been, ' Why not have gone to the Editor of
the "Phœnix"?' But my wife was touched by his
evident distress of mind and the idea of the invalid
in the waiting-room, and she gave him a sovereign
on loan.

I naturally looked upon that sovereign as lost.
It might indeed produce interest to my wife in
Paradise, where all good deeds are said to fructify ;
but so far as I was concerned I felt sure I should
never see either it or Mr. Henslow again.

The next morning, however, to my extreme

surprise, he called. A few words convinced me that he was the person he professed to be, and made me ashamed of my suspicions. 'Your wife's kindness,' he said, 'has enabled my sister to procure comfortable lodgings ; our return tickets were fortunately not in my lost purse, and now we are going back again.'

'But your sister has not seen the physician?'

'No,' he said with a faint flush; 'we must come up again for that.' Of course I understood that he referred to his want of cash, and forgetting in my turn, for the moment, that he might just as well apply to the 'Phœnix' as to me, I advanced him another loan. He accepted it with such modest hesitation as would have destroyed the last remnant of suspicion had any still survived within me, and, promising to return it by the next day's post, took his departure—for ever. No one that I know of has seen Mr. Henslow since. A week or so afterwards I called at the 'Phœnix' office, and found that I had not been imposed upon so far as his identity was concerned. He had, however, been paid beforehand for his serial story, and since then, as many callers testified, had levied contributions on the Charitable upon the strength of that literary achievement. If these lines should meet the gentle-

man's eye, I should like him to know that he
is forgiven, and that if he will only sit to me for
his character I should like to have further pecuniary dealings with him.   Such an idiosyncrasy as
his must be would be well worth my professional
attention.

The next greatest impostor I ever came across
was F——, the famous spiritualist.   Home being
on the Continent at the time (though an imperative
message from a court of law brought him shortly
afterwards to England), F—— was then at the head
of his profession in London, the very top of the
table-turners.   I met him for the first time at a
large party where there were many persons distinguished in literature ; not a few of whom, to my
great surprise, were believers in him.   I had
thoroughly investigated the spiritual business (for
copy), and knew it for what it was ; it has long
been exploded among all persons of intelligence,
and is now only represented by its bastard offspring,
thought-reading, but at that time it enjoyed considerable credit.   As I was known to be sceptical,
F—— undertook to tackle me.   He promised that
any dead friend of whom I should think would
indicate his presence in the usual manner—like a
postman.   F—— rapped out my friend's surname

accurately enough, though I did my best to delude
him by not hesitating at the proper letter, but he
was wrong in the Christian name. He made it
William instead of Henry, and I positively declined
to hear any communication from a departed spirit
who did not know the name given to him by his
godfathers and godmother. There was in fact a bit
of a row. The next day I mentioned the circumstance to H——, a common friend of mine and the
dead man's, and he at once said, 'But you were
wrong, my dear fellow; our friend's name *was*
William. It was his brother [whom we had also
known] who was Henry.'

The circumstance somewhat staggered both of
us, and we thought it only right, in justice to F——,
to let him know how the case stood. We accordingly called upon him in Seymour Street, where
he gave his *séances*, and I made my apology. He
was very dignified about it, and not at all
triumphant. 'I have no power over these things
myself,' he said; 'they are revealed to me; I am
merely an instrument' (and so he was, a stringed
one). He condescended so far, however, to combine
business with his 'mission' as to suggest a *séance*
then and there at a guinea a head, to which proposition we acceded.

I can see him now, a very fat, white-skinned man, with a face something like that of the first Napoleon, and I should think as great a scoundrel. His mode of procedure was to direct us to write down the names of a dozen dead friends on pieces of folded paper, and place them on the table. Then he would take one up in his large white hand, and inquire whether the spirit named therein was on the premises ; and, after two or three trials (for success was never achieved the first time), the re-ply came in the affirmative.   H——, though a man of great acquirements and intelligence, was of an exceptionally reverent nature, and he did not much like dealing with his dead friends so lightly ; but eventually he did what was required of him.   He wrote down, among others, the name of some one I had never heard of.   It was a woman's name—let us call it Lucy Lisle—and, of course, I was unaware that he had done so.   Suddenly the table at which we sat was violently perturbed—indeed, it was almost thrown upon us—and F——, in something like convulsions, raised his sleeve and displayed, written in letters of blood upon his arm, the words Lucy Lisle.

H——, greatly agitated, got up at once, and we left the house and took a walk together in Hyde

Park, where we discussed the matter. As luck would have it, there we met W. G. Clark, of Cambridge, and confided to him what had occurred, and he agreed to take a guinea's worth of supernatural information from F——, in my company, the next morning. What had happened, as we both agreed, was that the conjurer, while 'making hay,' as it were, of the dozen pieces of paper, had contrived to possess himself of one of them, and afterwards of its contents (this was afterwards found to be the case, but he had also a blank slip, which he dropped when he took up the other, so that there should always be the right number upon the table). What puzzled me, and delighted Clark, were the letters of blood.

The very same thing took place as on the former occasion. F—— pitched upon one of Clark's friends, and produced 'Henry James' upon his naked arm in gory characters.

'That is very curious,' said Clark in his dulcet tones. You have reproduced quite accurately the name that I wrote down; but I see that, by a mistake, no doubt arising from my official position (he was Tutor of Trinity at the time), 'I have written it with the surname first; the deceased gentleman's name was James Henry. That you have read my slip of paper is certain ; for that Mr. Henry, even in his disembodied state, should not know his surname from his Christian name is incredible. I shall not hesitate to say what has happened here wherever I go, and I should recommend you to leave London.'

F—— took this excellent advice within twenty-four hours. It was afterwards found, by experiment, that letters written by a stylus upon a white skin will remain, and apparently in blood, for more than a minute. It was certainly a very effective performance.

Among other eminent individuals imposed upon by this specious personage was the author of 'A Strange Story,' who was even reported to have said that 'if there had been no revelation, Mr. F—— would have convinced him of the existence of another world.' I had had some correspondence with Lord Lytton concerning Leitch Ritchie's pension, his claims to which he had (as it seemed to me curiously enough) refused to advocate upon the ground that he (his Lordship) was in opposition to Her Majesty's Government ; but the first time I met him was at the gathering at Knebworth in connection with the Guild of Literature and Art, which, though intended to become historical, was, to confess the truth, little short of a failure.

Some houses were built at Stevenage for the accommodation of decayed authors, in which none of them could be induced to live, even rent free. They pointed to the local train bills, and showed that it was impossible to reach their proposed homes after the performances at the theatres. This difficulty had not been taken into account by the patrons of the scheme, and there were others also—'What are you going to pay us for being buried alive at Stevenage?' for one.

The festival which was to inaugurate this new Arcadia of Literature was itself not a promising one. It was emphatically 'a scratch entertainment;' almost every author of eminence in London was invited to it, and a great many others; and 'the county' were asked to meet them. It was our host's idea to introduce these two classes to one another, so that, should any of the authors become 'decayed' (which was highly probable), they would be received with open arms by their landed neighbours. The two parties did not amalgamate. I was talking to Charles Collins, who with many others was staying in the house, when he was accosted by a fellow-guest of the 'exquisite' type. 'What a dem'd funny set of people!' he said ; ''pon my life, before I was told who they were, I thought it was *the Foresters.*'

Charles Collins, brother of the novelist of that name and son-in-law to Dickens, was himself an excellent writer. His 'Cruise upon Wheels' is one of the most charming books of travel ever written, and his short sketches—notably those two accounts of a visit to the Docks, one supposed to be written under local influences, and the other the next day in all statistical sobriety—testify to his great powers of humour. He was in weak health, and endured with admirable patience more physical suffering than his friends were aware of. He, however, sometimes exhibited a whimsical finicality. 'No one gives less trouble than myself,' he once observed to a friend of mine who was his host, 'but I like my little tastes consulted. Your bacon at breakfast is not very streaky, and *would* you be so kind as to ask your man to hang up my great coat by the loop ?'

I shall not easily forget his delight at the following little social *fiasco* which took place at the house of a dear, but somewhat fastidious, friend of ours in Westbourne Terrace. C——, a musical critic famous for his good dinners, happened to be calling at the same time as ourselves ; he, too, was fastidious, but in a much greater degree than our host, devoted to music, painting, and the fine arts, despising everyone who did not come up to his standard of culture, and I need hardly say, therefore, with a great horror of boys. Male children were smuggled away at his approach, lest they should put the accomplished creature out of tune. He was not in general very affable to anybody, but on this occasion he was exceptionally gracious, and especially to our host.

'My dear L——,' he exclaimed with effusion, 'are you engaged for Thursday week—Thursday, the twentieth ? If not, I have a nice little plan.' L—— dived into his breast-pocket for his engagement list. He scented the best of dinners, and also excellent company, none the worse for the circumstance that the host would sometimes retire to his bed to compose something (or perhaps himself) and leave them to their own devices.

'I am happy to say,' he answered, 'that on Thursday week I am free.'

'That is capital. Then on Thursday week I will come and dine with you.'

'Very good,' returned L——, though with a decided falling off in the enthusiasm of his manner.

S

'Yes, I will come, and I will bring with me— what do you think? a Bluecoat boy. The fact is, he proceeded to explain with an air of great relief and satisfaction, 'that I have promised his friends to see him into the mail train at Paddington, which is a long way from my house; while from Westbourne Terrace, you see, it would be no trouble to me at all.'

The whole scene, much embellished by the chagrined countenance of our host, formed one of the prettiest bits of genteel comedy I ever saw on the stage of real life.

A still droller incident of by no means a 'genteel' kind—since it implicated me in a very serious criminal offence—took place about this time. A great jewel robbery was committed at the West End under very ingenious circumstances. A gentleman and lady staying at a fashionable hotel had ordered a large quantity of valuable goods—chiefly diamonds—to be brought to them for their inspection. They drugged or chloroformed (I forget which) the jeweller's assistant who brought them, and got clear away with all the swag. It so happened that the whole adventure had been, as it were prefigured in 'Chambers's Journal' twelve months before; a contributor had imagined and written the incident just as it afterwards occurred, and the story had so recommended itself to some member of the criminal class that he had put it into practical execution. The jeweller thereupon wrote to the editor of the 'Journal' (poor me), charging him, not indeed with actual complicity with the crime, but as having been accessory to it before the fact. 'Under the pretence of elevating the masses,' he indignantly observed, 'you suggest to them ingenious methods of robbing honest tradesmen.' My answer to this gentleman was, I flatter myself, complete. I pointed out to him that if honest tradesmen would only read the respectable periodical I had the honour to edit—a moral duty not neglected, it seemed, even by the lowest classes—they would put themselves on their guard against such catastrophes. My position compelled me to appear to sympathise with the offenders, but I have always thought that they showed themselves miserably deficient in gratitude in never sending my contributor the least acknowledgment—not even one of the rings of which they had so many—for what he had done for them.

Their putting into practice the offspring of his imagination was certainly a curious thing to do. But Nature herself does not scorn to stoop to similar

acts of plagiarism. We story-tellers are often the
first to suggest an occurrence which, after it has actually happened, goes, most unjustly, to strengthen
the popular superstition that truth is stranger than
fiction.

Some years after the publication of ' Lost Sir
Massingberd ' the following paragraph appeared in
the ' Philadelphia Ledger : '—

'A Curious Discovery.—The hurricane which
passed over the Miami Valley on July 4 tore down a
number of old trees, and amongst them a large oak.
The owner of the property, a Mr. Rogers, on examining
the extent of the damage done by the storm, discovered in
the hollow of the fallen oak a human skeleton, with some
brass buttons and shreds of clothing, and among other
things a pocket-book with a number of papers. A communication to the " Miami County Democrat," signed J.
F. Clark, relates :—" The man's name, as gathered from
the papers, was Roger Vanderburg, a native of Lancaster,
Pennsylvania, and a captain in the Revolutionary Army.
He was an Aid to Washington during the retreat across
the Jerseys, and served a time in Arnold's head-quarters
at West Point. In 1791 he marched with St. Clair
against the North-western Indians, and in the famous
outbreak of that general on the Wabash, November 3 of
the year just written, he was wounded and captured.
But while being conveyed to the Indian town at Upper
Piqua he effected his escape, but found himself hard

pressed by his savage foes. He saw the hollow in the oak, and despite the mangled arm, and with the aid of a beech that grew beside the giant then, he gained the haven and dropped therein. Then came a fearful discovery. He had miscalculated the depth of the hollow, and there was no escape. Oh, the story told by the diary of the oak's despairing prisoner! How, rather than surrender to the torture of the stake, he chose death by starvation ; how he wrote his diary in the uncertain light and the snows! Here is one entry in the diary :— ' November 10.—Five days without *food*! When I sleep I dream of luscious fruits and *flowing* streams. The stars *laugh* at my misery! It is snowing now. I freeze while I starve. God *pity* me!' The italicised words were supplied by Mr. Rogers, as the trembling hand ofttimes refused to indite plainly. The entries covered a period of eleven days, and in disjointed sentences is told the story of St. Clair's defeat. Mr. Rogers has written to Lancaster to ascertain if any descendants of the ill-fated captain live ; if so, they shall have his bones." '

Again, in ' Murphy's Master,' I got rid of a great number of disagreeable characters on an island in the Indian Seas, by the simple, though startling, device of submerging the island itself ; the few respectable persons who inhabited it (including the hero and heroine) being most properly and providentially saved in a fishing-boat. Some critics thought it audacious ; but Nature was so favourably impressed by my little plan, that she used it herself two years afterwards, and in a more comprehensive way than I should have dared to invent ; an island in the Bay of Bengal, with the Kinshra lighthouse upon it, with seven scientific assistants, being submerged in a precisely similar manner.

I do not wish to be hard upon Nature, and, without giving details which could not but wound her *amour propre*, will merely remark that she committed a similar act of piracy in the case of my novel ' Found Dead.'

Though by no means a humorous story itself, that book, by the way, was the cause of a very fine stroke of humour. It was the custom with the very respectable firm of publishers with whom I did business at that time to pay my cheques to the names of my immortal works, instead of to myself; and since it suited their convenience so to do, I never complained of it, though it sometimes put me in rather a false position, when I presented my demands in person, as, for example, in the case of the ' Family Scapegrace.' When I came for the proceeds of ' Found Dead,' it was too much for the sense of (professional) propriety of the banker's clerk, who gravely observed, ' It is very fortunate, sir, that this cheque is not payable "to order,"

or it would have to be endorsed by your exe-
cutors.'

This incident, I remember, delighted Dickens,
who remarked, however, with a sudden access of
gravity, ' I should not like to have much money at a
bank which keeps so clever a clerk as that.'

He was himself an excellent man of business,
though in early life he made great pecuniary
mistakes by an impatience of disposition, a desire
to get things settled and done with, which is shared
by many men of letters to their great loss ; he was
painstaking, accurate, and punctual to a fault ; and
the trouble he took about other people's affairs,
especially in his own calling, is almost incredible.
Young men of letters are especially fortunate as
regards the sympathy and assistance they receive
from members of other professions. Almost all
of us have our Dr. Goodenough. The lawyers,
too, are always ready with their advice. I remember
mentioning a legal difficulty, which I had come
across in the plot of a novel, in the presence of one
who is now perhaps the foremost man at the
English bar. The next morning, though at that
time we had only a mere club acquaintance, I received from him half-a-dozen clearly written pages
explaining in the most lucid manner the law of the

case in point. The chiefs of our own calling
are always ready to give a helping hand to their
juniors ; but Dickens looked upon it as an imperative duty so to do.   Many a time have young
would-be contributors called upon me, and produced from their breast-pockets as passport to my
attention a letter of rejection, torn and frayed, and
bearing tokens of having been read a hundred
times, from the Master.

'He wrote me this letter himself,' they would
say, as though there were but one 'He' in the
world.   It was generally a pretty long one, though
written at a time when minutes were guineas to
him, full of the soundest advice and tenderest
sympathy.   There was always encouragement in
them (for of course these were not hopeless cases),
and often—whenever, in fact, there seemed need
for other help besides counsel—some allusion,
couched in the most delicate terms, to 'the enclosed.'   Dickens not only loved his calling, but
had a respect for it, and did more than any man
to make it respected.   With the pains he took
to perfect whatever proceeded from his own pen
everyone who has read his life must be conversant ;
but this minute attention to even the smallest
details had its drawbacks.   When an inaccuracy,

however slight, was brought home to him, it made him miserable. So conscious was I of this, that I never liked to tell him of a mistake in ' Dombey and Son,' which has escaped the notice of ' readers,' professional and otherwise, in every edition. The Major and Cleopatra sit down to play piquet ; but what they do play—for they ' propose to ' one another—is écarté.

In friendship, which in all other points must needs be frank and open, this problem often remains unsolved—namely, the friendship of one's friend for some other man. D. and E. have the most intimate relations with one another, but for the life of him E. cannot understand what D. sees in F. to so endear him to him. This was what many of D.'s (Dickens's) friends, and certainly the world at large, said of F. (John Forster). It is not my business, nor is it in my power, to explain the riddle ; I rarely met them together without witnessing some sparring between them—and sometimes without the gloves. On the other hand, I have known Forster pay some compliments to ' the Inimitable ' in his patronising way, which the other would acknowledge in his drollest manner. It is certain that Forster took the utmost interest in Dickens, even to the extent of seeing everything

he wrote through the press, and as to the genuineness of Dickens's regard for him I have the most
positive proof. I have already said that Dickens
once wrote to me spelling the word Foster (in
Foster Brothers) with an *r* ' because I am always
thinking of my friend Forster.' Long afterwards,
in acknowledging a service, which I had been fortunately able to do for him, in terms far more
generous than it deserved, he actually signed the
letter, not Charles Dickens, but John Forster !

When the biography of the former appeared,
and its editor was accused of representing himself
as standing in a nearer relation to Dickens than he
really was, I thought it only fair to Forster to send
him those two letters, with which—though, of
course, he had no need of the corroboration of such
a matter from without—he expressed himself
greatly pleased.

In 1871 I lost my old friend Robert Chambers,
and with it, after a short interval, the editorship of
the ' Journal.' My separation from it was a fore-
gone conclusion. My relations with the surviving
proprietor—always what the diplomatists call
' strained '—were severed within twelve months,
notwithstanding the good offices of his nephew,
Robert's son. My late contributors were so good

as to present me with a silver inkstand, suitably inscribed, which I value beyond any possession I have in the world. Their spokesman (a humorist) whispered as he handed it to me, 'Attenborough's is the place,' but it has never gone there.

My literary life from that time has gone on very smoothly—perhaps more smoothly than I deserve. I have been especially fortunate in finding friendship where I might naturally have only looked for business relations, nor do I believe that I have an enemy in my own calling, nor even among my 'natural foes,' the critics. On the other hand, I am well aware that there are a good many people who dislike me very cordially. If they do so for a good reason, I exceedingly regret it ; but there are some folks whose animosity is the highest of compliments. There is, in my opinion, no more fatal weakness in human nature than the desire to be thought well of by everybody.

When good fortune has once set in, the record of a man's life (especially a literary life) is apt to get uninteresting, and for that reason alone I should be disposed to end here, at all events for the present, what is after all rather a string of literary anecdotes (some of which, however, I venture to

think have some interest) than a literary autobiography. Moreover, the last decade of the life
of a living person is rather a delicate matter to
deal with.

It will be observed by those who have done me
the honour of reading them, that these reminiscences have scrupulously avoided all mention,
beyond a 'passing allusion,' to authors who are
happily still with us. I should have had nothing
but good to say of them, which would have sadly
disappointed some people, but in omitting them I
am well aware that I have deprived my narrative
of what would otherwise have been its chief
attraction. It is unambitious enough, Heaven
knows, and will interest, I fear, such persons only
as are interested in literary matters, and those but
of the lighter kind. It is, in fact, the literary
rather than the general public that I now address
—a reflection which causes me to add a few words
by way of postscript.

A personal experience to which I have already
alluded has taught me, 'by harsh evidence,' that
young persons who would embrace the literary
calling are very prompt to see its attractions and
very slow to understand its difficulties. From
the somewhat light and airy tone (of which no

one can be more conscious than myself) in which
these Recollections have been written, they may
conclude perhaps that the profession of literature
requires little pains or study, and that such a
moderate success at least as has been here described may be attained by a small amount of
work. I can only say, for my part, that when
I hear what are held to be hard-working men
in other callings talk of ' work,' I smile. I have
often found that what they mean by work (when
they are not in the enjoyment of a more or
less long vacation) is the remaining within the
same four walls for a certain large number of
hours *per diem.* Even when they do work, they
have something to work *upon* : they have not to
spin the very threads of their work out of their
own brains before they begin business. I have not
indeed been so close a prisoner as some of them,
for the necessities of my calling (so far as novel-
writing is concerned) have often compelled me to
seek change of scene, for 'local colouring ; ' but
for the last five-and-twenty years of my life I have
only had three days of consecutive holiday once a
year ; while all the year round (from another necessity of the pen) the Sundays have been as much
working days with me as the week days.

Such from day to day labours, though not, it is true, extending to long hours, would perhaps have been impossible but for the relief afforded by some favourite amusement ; this, in my case, as it has been in that of much greater men, has been the noble game of whist, which I have played regularly for two or three hours a day for the last thirty years. It does not, indeed, much matter what it is, so that the relaxation is an attractive one, but I pity that man from the bottom of my heart who can find no interest in a game. It is not everyone who, like Sarah Battle, can relax their minds over a book, and least of all those who write books. I have noticed that those of my own calling who read the most are not the best students of human nature, and fall most often into the pit of plagiarism. How often have I heard it said— too late—by those who have most certainly earned their play-time, ' How I wish I had an amusement!' The taste for such things must be caught early (like the measles) and indulged (like the patient) : what position, for example, is more unsatisfactory than that of the man who has only played whist occasionally—say once a week—and ' makes up a rubber to oblige'? In a partner's eyes, at least, such a person will never meet his obligations.

Mackworth Praed must have been a whist-player, or he never could have depicted ' Quince.'

> Some public principles he had,
>   But was no flatterer nor fretter ;
> He rapped his box when things were bad,
>   And said ' I cannot make them better.'
> And much he loathed the patriot's snort,
>   And much he scorned the placeman's snuffle,
> And cut the fiercest quarrel short,
>   With ' Patience, gentlemen,—and shuffle.'

Men of letters are rarely good card-players— Lord Lytton and Lever are almost the only exceptions I can call to mind—but some of them have been fond of whist, and have enlivened it by their sallies. A few of these, which I have happened myself to hear, seem worthy of record.

A guest being asked to a dinner party, which was to precede an evening at cards, thus apologised for coming in morning costume, ' The suit is surely no matter, so long as one is a Trump.'

A man who had his foot on a gout-rest was holding very bad cards, and complaining alike of his luck and his malady. Upon being reproached by his more fortunate adversary for his irritation, he suddenly exclaimed, ' It's all very well for *you*, but a "game hand" is a very different thing from a "game leg."'

On another occasion the same gentleman (whose temper, gout or no gout, was always a little short) jumped up from the seat where he had been losing and declared that he would play no more. 'But you'll break up the table,' pleaded the others pathetically. 'If it is broken up there will still be three "legs" left,' was his uncompromising reply.

A whist-player, who even though he was a loser ought to have known better than to have jested upon such a tender subject, once remarked with reference to the considerable number of novels for which I have been responsible, 'Nobody can deny, my dear fellow, that you have great "numerical strength."'[1]

I remember a little poem called 'Dumby,' written by a brother novelist, who has himself, alas! left a vacant place at the four-square table for ever, which has a pathetic singularity about it:

> I see the face of the friend I lost
>   Before me as I sit,
> His thin white hands, so subtle and swift,
>   And his eyes that gleam with wit.

---

[1] A term used to express plenty of small cards without an honour.

I see him across the square green cloth
 That's dappled with black and red ;
Between the luminous globes of light
 I watch the friend long dead.

It is only I who can see him there,
 With victory in his glance,
As, the cross ruff stopped, he strides along
 Like Wellington through France.

He died years past in the jungle reeds,
 But still I see him sit,
Facing me with his fan of cards,
 And those eyes that beam with wit.

In that excellent poem of Thomas Hood's in which he describes the village of Bullock Smithy, he exhibits a natural disinclination to come to the workhouse.

'There is one more house,'

he says,

'Which we have not come to yet, and I hope we never shall,
 And that's the Parish poorhouse.'

In these recollections of mine I feel a similar reluctance to allude to the Playhouse, for the fact

T

is my merits have never been recognised on the
boards. The subject is a sore one, and I will
merely say that when I think of a certain comedi-
etta called ' The Substitute,' and the way in which
it was treated by the dramatic critics, I appreciate
Landor's observation, made under similar circumstances in connection with his ' Imaginary Conver-
sations,' that he would bet a pint of porter that
none of his detractors, even if they took off their
coats to it, would come within a mile of them. ' The
Substitute ' ran for six weeks out of the season, at
the Court Theatre, and then I suppose ran right
away, for I have never heard of it since. It was
really one of the brightest—but there, as Tennyson
used (rather doubtfully) to be advertised to say
among the eulogistic criticisms on ' Festus,' ' I dare
not venture to say what I think about that play.'

If I have not been appreciated on the stage,
however, I have nothing to complain of in respect
to my reception off the boards.

The observation of a great writer on having
half-a-dozen bottles of brandy sent him by an
anonymous admirer is well known. ' This,' he said
with complacency, ' is true fame.' For my part, as
is only in accordance with the rules of proportion, I
have had to be content with much inferior liquor—

mere ginger-beer, a drink which is effervescent no doubt, but while it lasts is refreshing enough. I once lost a Persian cat, which (I had almost written who) was very dear to me, and I went to a suburban police office for professional advice as to handbills and rewards. 'What is your name, sir?' inquired the intelligent inspector. (It is cynically observed that inspectors are always called in the newspapers 'intelligent;' but this one, as will be seen, fully deserved the title.) As my business was a lawful one, I of course gave him no alias.

'James Payn?' he echoed. 'Are you the story-teller?'

I modestly murmured that I was.

'Then I tell you what,' he said, in a tone in which generosity and gratitude were finely blended, 'you are out of my district, but *I'll take the case.*'

And he took it. That was *my* brandy.

I have also had sums of money borrowed from me at various times by admirers of my genius— but that has given me less satisfaction.

PRINTED BY
SPOTTISWOODE AND CO., NEW-STREET SQUARE
LONDON